Community-Building Ideas

for Ministry with Young Teens

Diocesan Resource Center

1551 Tenth Avenue E

Seattle, WA 98102-0126

Heads-up | Easy | Low-Cost | Purposeful

Community-Building Ideas
for Ministry with Young Teens

Marilyn Kielbasa

Heads-up | Easy | Low-Cost | Purposeful

saint mary's press

The publishing team included Mary Duerson, copy editor; Barbara Bartelson, production editor; Hollace Storkel, typesetter; Cindi Ramm, art director; Kenneth Hey, cover and logo designer; cover images, PhotoDisc Inc.; produced by the graphics division of Saint Mary's Press.

The development consultants for the HELP (Heads-up, Easy, Low-Cost, and Purposeful) series included the following people:

Sarah Bush, Pewee Valley, Kentucky

Jeanne Fairbanks, Tipp City, Ohio

Carole Goodwin, Louisville, Kentucky

Joe Grant, Louisville, Kentucky

Maryann Hakowski, Belleville, Illinois

Jo Joy, Temple, Texas

Kevin Kozlowski, New Carlisle, Ohio

Jennifer MacArthur, Cincinnati, Ohio

David Nissen, Cincinnati, Ohio

Ruthie Nonnenkamp, Prospect, Kentucky

The activities in this book were created by the author and by the following contributors:

Joe Grant

Ruthie Nonnenkamp

The acknowledgments continue on page 204.

Printed in the United States of America

3404

ISBN 978-0-88489-571-8

Library of Congress Cataloging-in-Publication Data

Kielbasa, Marilyn
    Community-building ideas for ministry with young teens / Marilyn Kielbasa.
        p. cm.
    ISBN 978-0-88489-571-8 (pbk. : alk. paper)
        1. Church group work with teenagers. 2. Catholic youth—Religious life. I. Title.
    BX2347.8 .Y7 K54 2000
    259'.23—dc21
                                                                                    00-009549

Contents

Part C: Getting to Know One Another

Part D: Building Teams

Part E: Affirming One Another

Introduction

Community-Building Ideas for Ministry with Young Teens is one of seven books in the HELP series—a collection of **H**eads-up, **E**asy, **L**ow-Cost, and **P**urposeful activities for young adolescents. These strategies are designed to be used as part of a comprehensive youth ministry program for grades six to eight. The strategies can stand alone or complement a religious education curriculum.

The other books in the HELP series are as follows:

- *Family Ideas for Ministry with Young Teens*
- *Hands-on Ideas for Ministry with Young Teens*
- *Holiday and Seasonal Ideas for Ministry with Young Teens*
- *Justice and Service Ideas for Ministry with Young Teens*
- *Prayer Ideas for Ministry with Young Teens*
- *Retreat Ideas for Ministry with Young Teens*

These books are helpful resources for anyone who works with young adolescents in a church or school setting. They can provide a strong foundation for a year-round, total youth ministry program whose goal is to evangelize young adolescents and support them in their faith journey.

Overview of This Book

Community-Building Ideas for Ministry with Young Teens may be used by a coordinator of youth ministry, a director of religious education, catechists, teachers, a parish youth ministry team, or any adult who works with young teens. Ownership of the book includes permission to duplicate any part of it for use with program participants.

The book's strategies are organized into five sections:

◎ **Part A: Forming Small Groups** includes strategies to break down a large group into pairs or smaller groups in ways that are fun, objective, and non-threatening.

◎ **Part B: Gathering and Mingling** includes strategies to help young people learn one another's names and find out basic information about one another. This section also offers activities for teens to do alone or with one another during waiting times, such as before a session begins, during a break, or while waiting for meals on a retreat.

◎ **Part C: Getting to Know One Another** includes methods for taking a conversation between young teens to a deeper level, while preserving their need for boundaries and emotional safety.

◎ **Part D: Building Teams** provides outlines for several simulation games, process questions for follow-up discussion, and scriptural connections to help the young people see themselves and their peers connected to one another and to a faith community in a broader context through the Scriptures.

◎ **Part E: Affirming One Another** is a collection of strategies for building up the fragile self-images that often accompany the early-adolescent years. The activities also help young teens acquire the skill of giving compliments and encouragement to their peers.

Format of the Strategies

Each strategy begins with a brief description of its purpose. The next element is a suggested time for the activity. This is flexible and takes into account several variables, such as the size of the group, the comfort level of the participants, and whether you want to include a break. Use the suggested time as a starting point and modify it according to your circumstances. It is a good idea to include time for a break within the longer strategies.

Next is a description of the size of the group that the strategy was written for. Most of the strategies work with a range of group sizes. If your group is large, you may have to create smaller groups to conduct some of the activities, especially those outlined in part D on team building. Be sure to recruit enough adults to help with logistics and supervision. A good rule to follow is that for every six to eight young teens, one adult should be present.

In some strategies a section on special considerations follows the one on group size. It includes things such as cautions to pay special attention to a particular developmental issue of early adolescence.

A complete checklist of materials needed is the next part of the presentation of the strategy; this section is omitted if no materials are needed. A detailed description of the strategy's procedure is then provided, followed by alternative approaches. Those alternatives may be helpful in adapting the strategy to the needs of your group.

The strategies in part D and a few strategies in other parts of the book include a list of scriptural passages that may be used with the strategy, for reflection or prayer. The list is not exhaustive; a Bible concordance will provide additional citations if you want to add a more substantial scriptural component to a strategy.

The final element in each strategy offers space for keeping notes about how you might want to use the strategy in the future or change it to fit the needs of your group.

Programming Ideas

The strategies in this book can be used in a variety of ways. Consider the following suggestions:

- The program coordinator, catechists, teachers, and coordinator of youth ministry may collaborate to plan youth meetings and special activities that use strategies from this and other books in the HELP series.
- Schoolteachers may use ideas from this and other books in the HELP series to supplement their day-to-day curriculum.
- Many of the strategies in the HELP series can be adapted for use with multigenerational groups.

Standard Materials

Many of the items in the materials checklists are common to several strategies in the series. To save time consider gathering frequently used materials in convenient bins and storing those bins in a place that is accessible to all staff and volunteer leaders. Some recommendations for how to organize such bins follow.

Supply Bin
The following items frequently appear in materials checklists:

- Bibles, at least one for every two participants
- masking tape
- cellophane tape
- washable and permanent markers (thick and thin)
- pens or pencils
- self-stick notes
- scissors
- newsprint
- blank paper, scrap paper, and notebook paper
- postcards
- notepaper
- envelopes

◎ baskets

◎ candles and matches

◎ items to create a prayer space (e.g., a colored cloth, a cross, a bowl of water, and a vase for flowers)

Craft Bin

Many of the strategies use craft activities to involve the young people. Consider collecting the following supplies in a separate bin:

◎ construction paper

◎ yarn and string, in assorted colors

◎ poster board

◎ glue and glue sticks

◎ fabric paints

◎ glitter and confetti

◎ used greeting cards

◎ beads

◎ modeling clay

◎ paintbrushes and paints

◎ crayons

◎ used magazines and newspapers

◎ hole punches

◎ scissors

◎ stickers of various kinds

◎ index cards

◎ gift wrap and ribbon

Music Bin

Young people often find deep and profound meaning in the music and lyrics of songs, both past and present. Also, the right music can set an appropriate mood for a prayer or activity. Begin with a small collection of tapes or CDs in a music bin and add to it over time. You might ask the young people to put some of their favorite music in the bin. The bin might include the following styles of music:

◎ *Fun gathering music that is neither current nor popular with young teens.* Ideas are well-known classics (e.g., *Overture to William Tell, Stars and Stripes Forever,* and *1812 Overture*), songs from musical theater productions, children's songs, and Christmas songs for use any time of the year.

◎ *Prayerful, reflective instrumental music, such as the kind that is available in the adult alternative, or New Age, section of music stores.* Labels that specialize in this type of music include Windham Hill and Narada.

◎ *Popular songs with powerful messages.* If you are not well versed in popular music, ask the young people to offer suggestions.

◎ *The music of contemporary Christian artists.* Most young teens are familiar with Amy Grant, Michael W. Smith, and Steven Curtis Chapman. Also include the work of Catholic musicians, such as David W. Kauffman, Steve Angrisano, Bruce Deaton, Sarah Hart, Jesse Manibusan, and Jessica Alles.

Other Helpful Resources

In addition to the seven books in the HELP series, the following resources can be useful in your ministry with young adolescents.

For Team Building

Building Community in Youth Groups, by Denny Rydberg. Loveland, CO: Group Publishing, 1985.

Do It! by Thom Schultz and Joani Schultz. Loveland, CO: Group Publishing, 1989.

Youth Group Trust Builders, by Denny Rydberg. Loveland, CO: Group Publishing, 1993.

From Saint Mary's Press

All the books in the following list are published by Saint Mary's Press and can be obtained by calling or writing us at the phone number and address listed in the "Your Comments or Suggestions" section at the end of this introduction.

Catechism Connection for Teens series, by Lisa Calderone-Stewart and Ed Kunzman (1999).
    That First Kiss and Other Stories
    My Wish List and Other Stories
    Better Than Natural and Other Stories
    Straight from the Heart and Other Stories
    Meeting Frankenstein and Other Stories
    The five books in this collection contain short, engaging stories for teens on the joys and struggles of adolescent life, each story with a reflection connecting it to a Catholic Christian belief. Each book's faith connections reflect teachings from a different part of the *Catechism of the Catholic Church.*

The Catholic Youth Bible, edited by Brian Singer-Towns (2000). The most youth-friendly Bible for Catholic teens available. The scriptural text is accompanied by hundreds of articles to help young people pray, study, and live the Scriptures.

Faith Works for Junior High: Scripture- and Tradition-Based Sessions for Faith Formation, by Lisa-Marie Calderone-Stewart (1993). A series of twelve active meeting plans on various topics related to the Scriptures and church life.

Guided Meditations for Junior High: Good Judgment, Gifts, Obedience, Inner Blindness, by Jane E. Ayer (1997). Four guided meditations for young teens, available on audiocassette or compact disc. A leader's guide includes the

script and programmatic options. Other volumes in this series, called A
Quiet Place Apart, will also work with young teens.

Looking Past the Sky: Prayers by Young Teens, edited by Marilyn Kielbasa (1999).
A collection of 274 prayers by and for young adolescents in grades six to
eight.

One-Day Retreats for Junior High Youth, by Geri Braden-Whartenby and Joan Finn
Connelly (1997). Six retreats that each fit into a school day or an afternoon
or evening program. Each retreat contains a variety of icebreakers, prayers,
group exercises, affirmations, and guided meditations.

Prayers with Pizzazz for Junior High Teens, by Judi Lanciotti (1996). A variety of
creative prayer experiences that grab young teens' attention. The prayers
are useful in many different settings, such as classes, meetings, prayer
services, and retreats.

ScriptureWalk Junior High: Bible Themes, by Maryann Hakowski (1999). Eight
90-minute sessions to help bring youth and the Bible together. Each session
applies biblical themes to the life issues that concern young teens.

Connections to the Discovering Program

The Discovering Program, published by Saint Mary's Press, is a religious education program for young people in grades six to eight. It consists of fourteen six-
session minicourses. Each session is 1 hour long and based on the principles of
active learning.

The strategies in the HELP series cover themes that are loosely connected
to those explored in the Discovering Program, and can be used as part of a
total youth ministry program in which the Discovering curriculum is the central
catechetical component. However, no strategy in the series presumes that the
participants have taken a particular course in the Discovering Program, or requires that they do so. The appendices at the end of this book list the connections between the HELP strategies and the Discovering courses.

Your Comments or Suggestions

Saint Mary's Press wants to know your reactions to the strategies in the HELP
series. We are also interested in new youth ministry strategies for use with young
teens. If you have a comment or suggestion, please write the series editor, Marilyn
Kielbasa, at 702 Terrace Heights, Winona, MN 55987-1320; call the editor at our
toll-free number, 800-533-8095; or e-mail the editor at *mkielbasa@smp.org.*
Your ideas will help improve future editions of these books.

Part A
Forming Small Groups

The strategies in part A can be used to divide a large group of young people into smaller groups. Such activities are often called groupers. Using groupers can help build community because many of them direct the participants to mix with people outside of their regular group of friends. Grouping activities also preserve the emotional safety in a group of young teens by allowing the small groups to form objectively rather than by personal choices based on popularity.

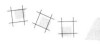

It's a Match

OVERVIEW

This grouping activity randomly creates pairs by assigning everyone half of a famous duo, fictional or historical, and directing them to find someone holding the match to their person.

Suggested Time

About 10 minutes, depending on the size of the group

Group Size

This strategy can be done with any size group.

Materials Needed

- ☼ one copy of resource 1, "Famous Pairs," cut apart as scored
- ☼ a scissors
- ☼ a bowl or a bag

PROCEDURE

Preparation. Resource 1 provides thirty famous pairs that are likely to be known by young people. Select the pairs that you would like to use and mix up those name slips in a bowl or a bag. Set aside the rest for future use. If you have more than sixty young people, think of other famous pairs that are popular with them and write name slips for each of those people or characters. You might use the names of characters on television shows that the young people watch, local personalities, or characters from popular video games.

Let the young people each draw a name slip from the bowl or the bag of slips that you prepared. If you have an odd number of participants, ask one adult leader to take part in the activity. When everyone has a name, explain the process as follows:

When I give a signal, start looking for the match to your famous person or fictional character. For example, if the name on your slip of paper is Adam, you should look for Eve. If you have Mickey Mouse, you should look for Minnie Mouse.

When you find your partner, sit down with that person and wait for the next instructions.

When you are sure that the young people understand the task, give a signal to start. You may need to help some people figure out who their match is.

ALTERNATIVE APPROACHES

◎ If you have a large group and suspect that the process might take a while, give a common task to each pair as soon as they find each other. You might give them a puzzle to do, such as one of those found in part B of this book. An immediate task can reduce feelings of discomfort between people who do not know each other.

◎ Use this strategy as a focusing activity for a biblical lesson by creating pairs of biblical characters. Use it as a focusing activity for a lesson on media by creating pairs of famous television partners.

◎ Rather than forming pairs, form groups of three or four people by creating your own list of famous trios or quartets. Some examples follow: Peter, James, John; Donald Duck, Goofy, Pluto; Charlie Brown, Lucy, Linus, Snoopy; Teresa of Ávila, Joan of Arc, Elizabeth Seton, Frances Cabrini

◎ Instead of giving each person a slip of paper with a name, write the names on self-stick name tags. Distribute the name tags when the young people arrive and direct them to wear the tags in a prominent location on their clothing for the opening activity.

◎ If you plan to distribute folders or books to everyone as part of the gathering, tape a name in an unobtrusive place in each folder or book before the session. When it is time for the grouping activity, direct the young people where to look for their person or character. You might also tape the names underneath chairs ahead of time.

NOTES

Use the space below to jot notes and reminders for the next time you use this strategy.

(This strategy is adapted from *More Attention Grabbers for Fourth–Sixth Graders,* by David Lynn, p. 21.)

Famous Pairs

Kermit the Frog	**Pat Sajak**	**Adam**
Miss Piggy	**Vanna White**	**Eve**
Bert	**Batman**	**David**
Ernie	**Robin**	**Goliath**
Dorothy	**Charlie Brown**	**Elmer Fudd**
Toto	**Lucy Van Pelt**	**Bugs Bunny**
Winnie the Pooh	**Snoopy**	**Garfield**
Tigger	**Woodstock**	**Odie**
Piglet	**Mickey Mouse**	**Abraham**
Eeyore	**Minnie Mouse**	**Sarah**

| Lucille Ball | Barbie | Fred Flintstone |
| Desi Arnaz | Ken | Wilma |

| Quasimodo | Romeo | Pocahontas |
| Esmerelda | Juliet | John Smith |

| Paul | Jack | Sylvester |
| Barnabas | Jill | Tweety |

| Ariel | Scarecrow | Harry Potter |
| Prince Eric | Tinman | Ron Weasley |

| Mary | Buzz Lightyear | Simba |
| Joseph | Woody | Nala |

Comic Strip Capers

OVERVIEW The young people form small groups by finding other people who have complementary panels of a comic strip.

Suggested Time

About 10 minutes, depending on the size of the group

Group Size

This strategy works best with groups larger than ten people.

Materials Needed

- ☀ several comic strips from newspapers, with the panels cut apart, one panel for each person
- ☀ a scissors
- ☀ paper clips
- ☀ cellophane tape, one roll for each small group (optional)

PROCEDURE

Preparation. Gather a variety of comic strips from newspapers. Cut apart the panels of each strip and clip them together. Separate the strips into piles, according to the number of panels in each. Most daily strips have two to four panels; Sunday strips often have more. Keep in mind that the number of panels will determine the size of the small groups that are formed when you do this activity. So, for example, if you want three-person groups, use three-panel comic strips.

1. Get an accurate count of the young people as they arrive, and decide which of the comic strips that you prepared will be used to create the groups. For example, if you have twenty-six participants, you may want to use five four-panel strips and two three-panel strips.

2. Unclip the comic strip panels that you have decided to use, mix them up, and distribute them randomly among the participants. Tell the young people that their task is to find the other people whose panels, when combined with theirs, complete a comic strip. When they have accomplished the task, direct them to sit down with their small-group members and wait until all the strips are complete.

You might give each small group a roll of cellophane tape and tell the group members to tape their strip together. The re-formed strip can be used to label a group task; for example, if the groups' next task is to create a newsprint list, they could each tape their strip to their work. Or for the remainder of the meeting, you could refer to the groups by their comic strip's name.

ALTERNATIVE APPROACH

◎ To make the task more difficult, use different installments of the same comic strip. For example, cut up the panels from different "Hi and Lois" strips and tell the participants to find the panels that go with their piece. This alternative works especially well with smaller groups, where the task of finding complementary panels of different comic strips may not be challenging enough to be fun.

NOTES

Use the space below to jot notes and reminders for the next time you use this strategy.

(This strategy is adapted from *More Attention Grabbers for Fourth–Sixth Graders,* by David Lynn, pp. 25–26.)

It's in the Cards

This strategy uses playing cards to form groups of any number of sizes.

Suggested Time

About 5 minutes, depending on the size of the group

Group Size

This grouper works best with groups of eight or more participants. If you have more than fifty-two participants, use a second deck of cards.

Materials Needed

- a deck of playing cards
- double-stick tape (optional)

PROCEDURE

Preparation. Count out enough playing cards so that each participant gets a card that fits into a grouping sequence. For example, if you have twenty participants and you want groups of four, you could use all the cards from ace through five.

1. As the young people arrive, give each of them a playing card and tell them to keep it in a safe place. You may want to have them attach the card to their clothing with double-stick tape.

2. Choose one of the following methods to direct the participants into small groups:

- Tell everyone to gather with people holding cards of the same suit as their card. You can limit the number in a group by saying something like, "Form groups of five by gathering with four other people whose cards are in the same suit as yours."
- Have everyone gather with people holding cards of the same number or figure (jack, queen, or king) as their card. If you are using only one deck of cards or a partial deck, this method will result in groups of four or fewer.
- Before the session put together a deck of cards with one or more examples of a common poker hand. For example, if you have twenty participants and you would like them to form four groups of five, you might create a deck of cards with four straights (five-card sequences), straight flushes (five-card sequences in the same suit), or full houses (two of a kind and three of a kind). After distributing the cards, call out the hand you have chosen, and tell the young people to gather with others to create that combination.
- Gather the participants according to odd numbered, even numbered, or face cards.
- Form pairs by having the young people find a matching number or figure.
- Create groups with numbers that add up to a designated number. If you are using face cards, count them as ten points. For example, you might tell the young people to form groups by finding people whose cards, along with their own, add up to twenty-five. A group might consist of five people holding a five, a two, a nine, a six, and a three. If you use this method, the number of participants in each group will vary.

ALTERNATIVE APPROACHES

⊚ Use the playing cards as name tags. Write each person's name in big, bold letters on a separate playing card so that it is easy to read. Attach a safety pin or double-stick tape to the back of the card.

⊚ Once the groups are formed, use the playing card mixer "Number, Please" from part B of this manual, or "Suits Me!" from part C.

NOTES

Use the space below to jot notes and reminders for the next time you use this strategy.

(This strategy is adapted from *Attention Grabbers for Fourth–Sixth Graders,* by David Lynn, pp. 26–27.)

Shoe Search

This strategy has the young people form groups by finding their shoes in piles of shoes that you have created randomly, and joining with others whose shoes were in the same pile.

Suggested Time

About 5 minutes, depending on the size of the group

Group Size

This activity works best with between ten and forty people.

Special Considerations

Young teens are frequently self-conscious about their body. This grouper might be uncomfortable for some of them because it involves revealing a part of the body that may be a source of embarrassment. For example, some young people may be embarrassed by foot odor; others may be reluctant to reveal holes in their socks or socks that do not match. It is best to use this grouper with people who know one another well or are comfortable enough with one another that they will not experience a high degree of anxiety.

PROCEDURE

1. Gather the young people in a circle. Ask them to remove their right shoe and put it in the center of the circle.

2. When everyone has done this, randomly choose the same number of shoes as you want people in a small group. Display the shoes to the group, and put them in the area in which the small group will meet. Do this for each group of shoes.

3. When you have finished dividing the shoes, tell the young people to go to the area where their shoe is located. They may then put on their shoe.

NOTES

Use the space below to jot notes and reminders for the next time you use this strategy.

Let's Make a Sandwich

OVERVIEW

The young people form groups by gathering with other people to make a "sandwich."

Suggested Time

About 5 minutes, depending on the size of the group

Group Size

This grouper works best with a minimum of twelve people.

Materials Needed

- a copy or copies of resource 2, "Sandwich Ingredients," cut apart as scored
- a scissors
- newsprint and markers
- masking tape

PROCEDURE

Preparation. Decide how many people you want in each group and for each group cut out a set of ingredients from resource 2, using only as many ingredients as group members. For example, if you want six people in each group, eliminate two ingredients. Cut out a few extra ingredients so that you have some flexibility in forming groups if needed.

List on a sheet of newsprint the ingredients that you have chosen to make up a sandwich. Post the newsprint and cover it until it is needed.

1. Randomly distribute the ingredient slips, one to each person. If the group does not divide evenly by the number you have chosen for the group size, use as many of the extra ingredient slips as you need to make sure that everyone has one.

2. Display the newsprint list of ingredients that you created before the session. Direct the young teens to make a sandwich by gathering with other people who have complementary ingredients.

ALTERNATIVE APPROACHES

◎ Form groups by making pizzas, banana splits, tacos, or another teen favorite. Create a master list such as the one in resource 2.

◎ If you plan to distribute folders or books to everyone as part of the gathering, tape a sandwich ingredient in an unobtrusive place in each folder or book before the session. When it is time for the grouping activity, direct the young people where to look for their ingredient. You might also tape the ingredients underneath chairs ahead of time.

◎ Form pairs or groups of two or three by using food combinations such as peanut butter and jelly; bacon, lettuce, and tomato; or spaghetti and meatballs.

◎ If you are using this grouper in a format where you will be providing a meal or a snack, provide food that corresponds to the item the groups create. For example, provide the ingredients for sandwiches or tacos, order pizzas, or create the "world's longest banana split."

For the banana split, have on hand the necessary ingredients and a section of rain gutter purchased at a building supply store to serve as the dish. Be sure to wash out the gutter with hot water before using it. Let everyone participate in creating the ice cream concoction.

NOTES

Use the space below to jot notes and reminders for the next time you use this strategy.

Sandwich Ingredients

bread	bread	bread
ham	ham	ham
cheese	cheese	cheese
lettuce	lettuce	lettuce
tomato	tomato	tomato
mustard	mustard	mustard
mayonnaise	mayonnaise	mayonnaise
pickle	pickle	pickle

bread	bread	bread
ham	ham	ham
cheese	cheese	cheese
lettuce	lettuce	lettuce
tomato	tomato	tomato
mustard	mustard	mustard
mayonnaise	mayonnaise	mayonnaise
pickle	pickle	pickle

Phrase Match

The participants form groups by reconstructing a popular saying, song title, or scriptural verse.

Suggested Time

About 10 minutes, depending on the size of the group

Group Size

This strategy works best with groups of ten or more.

Materials Needed

☼ slips of paper, one for each person
☼ a pen
☼ small prizes (optional)
☼ cellophane tape (optional)

PROCEDURE

Preparation. Brainstorm popular sayings, song titles, or scriptural verses, as many as the number of small groups you want to form. You may want to tailor these to the content of what follows in your session (several examples follow). Divide each saying, song title, or verse into words and phrases equal to the number of people you want in each group. Write each word or phrase on a separate slip of paper (if you use any from the list below, do not include the bracketed note after each); clip together the pieces of each saying, song, or verse; and label each batch of slips with the number of slips in it. This will enable you to determine later which combination of sayings and verses to use in order to be sure everyone gets a slip. You may want to make up a few more sets than you think you will need, in a variety of sizes, to accommodate any number of participants.

For a session on friendship
◎ "A friend in need is a friend indeed" [English proverb].
◎ "Love is patient; love is kind; love is not envious or boastful" [1 Cor. 13:4].
◎ "Love one another as I have loved you" [John 15:12].
◎ "The only way to have a friend is to be one" [Ralph Waldo Emerson].

For a class on the Eucharist
◎ "Do this in memory of me."
◎ "I am the bread of life" [John 6:35].
◎ "He had been made known to them in the breaking of the bread" [Luke 24:35].
◎ "This is my body. This is my blood."

For a meeting during Advent
◎ "Prepare the way of the Lord, / make his paths straight" [Matt. 3:3].
◎ "O Come, O Come, Emmanuel" [song title]
◎ "Hail, favored one! The Lord is with you" [Luke 1:28, NAB].
◎ "The voice of one crying out in the wilderness" [Matt. 3:3].

1. Determine the number of people participating and select which sets of paper slips you will use so that each person gets one slip. Randomly distribute the slips of paper, one to each participant. Tell the young people to find the other people who hold words or phrases that when combined with theirs make up a familiar saying, song title, or Scripture verse. Explain that when they think they have found everyone in their group, the group members should put the slips in order and read the saying or verse aloud together. You may want to award small prizes for the first group to complete the task.

2. If you like, direct the groups to tape together the pieces of their saying or verse and post it near their small-group meeting space.

ALTERNATIVE APPROACHES

◎ If you have a large group, it might be helpful to write all the sayings on a sheet of newsprint so that the participants have a clue about what words or phrases they are looking for.

◎ Before the session assign each participant to a particular group, write a name tag for each person, and separate the name tags into the groups you have assigned. Then, using a different saying, song, or verse for each group, write a word or phrase on each person's name tag. This way when you distribute the name tags and tell everyone to search for the other words and phrases that go with their slip, they will form the groups that you planned on.

◎ Use all songs titles or all lyrics. If you use lyrics, instruct the participants to form a group by reconstructing the song and singing it together.

NOTES

Use the space below to jot notes and reminders for the next time you use this strategy.

(This strategy is adapted from *Attention Grabbers for Fourth–Sixth Graders*, by David Lynn, pp. 23–24.)

Word Clumps

The young people are each assigned a letter, and then they form groups by forming words. This activity can be used several times in a meeting to mix and remix the participants.

Suggested Time

About 5 minutes, depending on the size of the group. However, this activity could take longer if you use it as a mixer and do it several times.

Group Size

This activity works best with a large group.

Materials Needed

- 3-by-5-inch index cards
- markers

PROCEDURE

Preparation. Write one letter of the alphabet on an index card for each person. You may repeat letters—especially vowels—and you may avoid less frequently used letters such as *H, K, J, Q, W, X,* and *Z.* Be sure that the cards you end up with have enough flexibility to construct a variety of words. You might want to consult a Scrabble game for hints on frequency of letters.

1. Give each participant one of the index cards you prepared. Explain to everyone that you will announce a number and they are to form words made up of the same number of letters as the number you call out. You may want to set some guidelines, such as no proper names and no foreign words.

2. Begin by calling out a relatively low number, such as four or five, and give a signal to start. When the participants form a word, they are to shout it out together and sit down. You are likely to have some young people left over after the words have been formed. Have them form a group by themselves.

3. To use this activity as a mixer, go through the same process as often as time allows, changing the number each time (use higher numbers for more of a challenge). You may want to give the first groups to form a short question to answer while they are waiting for everyone else to form words. If the group members do not know one another, this would be a good time to share names, schools, grade levels, hobbies, and so forth.

ALTERNATIVE APPROACHES

◎ If you have a large group, hold up a large, bold number card corresponding to the number you call out. This will help those who may not be able to hear you.

◎ Attach a seasonal or a learning connotation to the activity. For example, challenge the participants to form words that have to do with Easter or the Scriptures, or have them form the names of saints.

◎ To further develop this strategy as a community builder, challenge the entire group to create a giant crossword puzzle, somewhat like the word game Scrabble, by arranging their small-group words in intersecting horizontal and vertical lines. This can be done by laying the index card letters on the floor, or by having the young people line up with their letter.

NOTES

Use the space below to jot notes and reminders for the next time you use this strategy.

Cereal Box Puzzles

The young teens create groups by putting together puzzles created from the fronts of empty cereal boxes.

Suggested Time

About 5 minutes, depending on the size of the group

Group Size

This strategy works well with at least fifteen people.

Materials Needed

- several empty cereal boxes, one for each small group and a few extras
- a scissors
- large paper clips
- cellophane tape or masking tape, one roll for each small group
- blank self-stick name tags, one for each person
- markers, one for each person

PROCEDURE

Preparation. Decide what size you want the small groups to be. Divide the expected number of participants by the ideal size of the small groups and round up. That is the number of different cereal boxes you will need, plus a few extra boxes if you might have more participants. Cut up the fronts of the cereal boxes into the same number of pieces as your ideal group size, and clip together the pieces from each box.

1. When you know how many participants you have, select enough puzzles so that each person can receive one piece. Mix up the pieces of those puzzles and randomly distribute one to each person. (If you have pieces left over, hang on to them until later.) Explain to the participants that their task is to reconstruct the front of a cereal box by finding the other people who have pieces to the same front.

2. As the groups form, give each one a roll of cellophane tape or masking tape, and enough name tags and markers for everyone in the group. Direct the groups to tape together their box front. If you are holding extra puzzle pieces, distribute them so that every group can complete its puzzle. Then have everyone make and put on a name tag with their first name, the name of their group's cereal, and their last name, such as Maria Cheerios Baxter or William Fruit Loops Collano.

ALTERNATIVE APPROACHES

◎ To make the task more difficult, use the same type of cereal box for everyone, but be sure to vary how you cut out each box front. If you use this option, eliminate the name tags or give out premade ones as people arrive. This is a good alternative to use if you are forming pairs or triads and cutting each box front into only two or three pieces.

◎ Another way to make the task more difficult: For each box front, cut out a mystery piece, that is, a piece that does not look like the others. You might use a piece that shows only the brand name, or a corner, and so forth.

◎ Use something besides cereal boxes to create the puzzles. You may want to tie the puzzles into a theme. For example, use empty detergent boxes to tie in to a session about the sacrament of Reconciliation (also called Penance), old birthday cards to begin a lesson on using the gifts God gave to each of us, or magazine covers as part of a study of media.

NOTES

Use the space below to jot notes and reminders for the next time you use this strategy.

Lego Puzzler

OVERVIEW	The participants form groups by copying a structure you have created out of Lego blocks.

Suggested Time

About 10 minutes, depending on the size of the group and the size of the structure you create

Group Size

This strategy works best with groups of six through thirty.

Materials Needed

- ☼ a variety of Legos
- ☼ zipper sandwich bags, one for each person
- ☼ small prizes (optional)

PROCEDURE

Preparation. Create something out of Legos. The simpler the item is, the less time it will take for the small groups to reproduce it.

Decide how many small groups you will need. Make one pile of Legos for each small group. Each pile should contain exactly the same number and type of items you used in your Lego creation. It will simplify matters greatly if you use the same colors in each pile that you used in your creation. For example if you used three square black bricks, four rectangular red bricks, a blue single-line brick, and two wheels in your creation, you should put those same items in each pile.

Decide how many people will be in each small group. Divide the items in each pile by that number, place each smaller pile in a zipper sandwich bag, and seal the bag. Make sure you have one bag for each participant.

1. Distribute the bags of Legos among the participants. Show them your Lego creation and explain that their task is to find the people whose bag contains the pieces necessary to reproduce the structure. Let them know how many people are in each small group so they know when they have a complete set of pieces. Explain to the young people that when their small group is complete, they are to reproduce the Lego structure as quickly as possible, but they may come up and examine the model only one time, together.

2. When all the groups have finished, compare the results to the original model. You may want to award small prizes to the members of the group that finished first, the group that came closest to the original model, and so forth.

ALTERNATIVE APPROACHES

◎ This activity works equally well with toy-building materials other than Legos.
◎ To use this activity as a team builder, create a bigger structure and give each participant more pieces. You may want to number the bags in a way that the young teens know which group they belong to. Or you can use a simple method of creating groups, even predefine them, and just give each team the necessary Legos. You might also increase the number of times they can examine the structure.
◎ If you have a large group, construct several identical toy structures and place them around the room for reference. Again, you may want to number the bags in a way that tells the young teens which group they belong to.

NOTES

Use the space below to jot notes and reminders for the next time you use this strategy.

Preferences Name Tags

The young people identify certain preferences on their name tags. When it is time to form small groups, the participants gather with others who expressed the same preference in a category that the leader calls out. This strategy works best if you have several small-group activities planned and want to form different groups each time.

Suggested Time

About 10 minutes to make the name tag and 1 or 2 minutes more each time you form small groups

Group Size

This strategy works with any size group.

Materials Needed

- ☼ 4-by-6-inch or 5-by-8-inch index cards, one for each person
- ☼ a variety of markers
- ☼ newsprint
- ☼ masking tape
- ☼ pieces of double-stick tape, straight pins, or safety pins, one for each person

PROCEDURE

Preparation. Decide how many times you will regroup the participants, and how many small groups you will need. Then identify a category for each regrouping, and a set of items for each category. For example, if you will regroup four times and need six small groups, identify four categories with six items in each. You may select categories and items from the list below, modifying them as necessary to suit your needs, or create your own. Always include the item "other or none" for those who have no preference.

Next create a mockup of a name tag on newsprint, positioning the paper horizontally. In the middle write, "Name," in large letters. Then write the categories and their items on separate sections of the newsprint. For example, if you have four categories, you might write each category and its items in a separate corner of the newsprint. Post the sample name tag in a prominent place.

Favorite Sesame Street *character*

- Bert
- Ernie
- Big Bird
- Oscar
- Cookie Monster
- Elmo
- other or none

Favorite childhood superhero

- Batman
- Batgirl
- Spiderman
- Ninja Turtles
- Power Rangers
- Xena, the Warrior Princess
- other or none

Favorite flavor of ice cream

- vanilla
- chocolate
- strawberry
- cookie dough
- rocky road
- chocolate chip
- other or none

Favorite sports team
[List college or professional teams that are popular in your area. Include a category that says something like, "not into sports."]

Favorite candy

- Hershey's bar
- Snickers
- Skittles
- Reese's peanut butter cups
- Starburst
- other or none

Favorite childhood cartoon or children's show
[List cartoons and children's shows that were popular in your area six or seven years ago. Include the category "other or none."]

1. Give each young person an index card. Provide a variety of markers. Display the sample name tag that you created on newsprint. Direct the young teens to write their name in the center of their index card. Then, referring to the name-tag poster that you posted, tell them to choose one selection from each category and write their choices on the corresponding section of their index card. Distribute pieces of double-stick tape, straight pins, or safety pins, and tell everyone to put on their name tag.

2. When it is time to form small groups, announce a category from the sample name tag, for example, "Favorite flavor of ice cream," and tell the young people to gather with other people who made the same selection as they did for that category. At another time during the class or meeting, when you want to re-form the small groups, call out another category and have everyone regather.

ALTERNATIVE APPROACH

◎ Use this activity as a simple get-to-know-you exercise instead of a grouping activity. To do so, do not list possibilities on the sample name tag. Just list the categories, like, "Favorite childhood superhero" or "Favorite color," and let people write in what they want.

NOTES

Use the space below to jot notes and reminders for the next time you use this strategy.

Release Me Relay

This activity begins with everyone seated and frozen on the floor. None of the seated people can communicate, except with their eyes. Team captains are randomly chosen, and they in turn race to assemble their teams by releasing people from their spot on the floor.

Suggested Time

About 10 minutes, depending on the size of the group

Group Size

This activity works best with groups of fifteen or more.

Materials Needed

- ☼ small pieces of paper
- ☼ markers
- ☼ a paper bag or a box
- ☼ small prizes (optional)

PROCEDURE

1. As the participants arrive, have each of them write their name on a piece of paper. Place all the names in a bag or a box and put it aside until you are ready to use it.

2. Direct everyone to sit on the floor and explain that they must remain seated and still, as if stuck to the floor, until they are released by their team. They cannot talk or gesture. They can communicate only with their eyes.

3. Decide how many small groups you will need. Choose that many names from the bag or the box and designate those people as the team captains. Explain that they are each to randomly choose a name from the bag or the box and find that person. The person cannot talk, gesture, or move from her or his spot on the floor until the team captain touches her or him on the head. When that happens the person is released and becomes the captain's assistant. She or he is now free to talk and move around. Together the captain and the assistant go back to the bag, where the captain chooses another name. They must find that person and both the captain and the assistant must tap her or him on the head. Then all three go to the bag, choose one more name, and follow the same procedure. Each time, the person being sought cannot talk, gesture, or leave the floor until she or he has been tapped by all the team members. Continue in this manner until the groups are formed.

You may want to award small prizes to the group that is formed first, the team member who best communicated with his or her eyes, and so forth.

ALTERNATIVE APPROACHES

⊚ If you think the young teens would be comfortable doing so, tell them to link arms with each new team member as that person is released, forming a human chain.

⊚ If you are using name tags for your gathering, use this activity to distribute them. Have everyone write their name on a tag instead of a piece of paper, and put the tags in a bag or a box. When you choose team captains, let them put on their name tag. Direct them to put a name tag on each new team member as part of the ritual that releases him or her from the floor.

NOTES

Use the space below to jot notes and reminders for the next time you use this strategy.

A Baker's Dozen Short Groupers

OVERVIEW Each of these thirteen strategies is a quick way to gather young teens into small groups. Each one is nonthreatening, easy to do, objective, safe, and fun.

Suggested Time

Most of these groupers can be done in 5 minutes or less, depending on the size of the group.

Group Size

These activities work with any size group.

Materials Needed

Aside from "Stick Out Your Tongue," which requires lollipops or hard candy, the activities below require nothing more than you would normally have available for a gathering of young teens: pens or pencils, markers, newsprint, masking tape, and so forth.

Happy Birthday

Before the gathering write each of the twelve months of the year on a separate piece of paper. Post the papers around the room. Direct the teens to gather under the month they were born. If the groups are drastically uneven, ask some people to move to a different group.

Number, Please

Write each of the numbers 0 through 9 on a separate piece of paper. Post the papers around the room. When the time comes for breaking into groups, direct the young people to gather under the number that is the last digit of their phone number.

Four Seasons

Write the name of each of the four seasons on a separate sheet of paper. Post the papers around the room. Tell the young people to gather under the name of the season during which they were born. You may need to identify the calendar definitions of when each season begins.

Stick Out Your Tongue

As the young people arrive, give them each a lollipop or a piece of hard candy. Tell them to suck on the candy until the session begins. When it is time to break into small groups, do so by tongue colors. You can also do this grouper by giving each person a certain color of bubblegum ball and asking them to chew the gum and blow bubbles. Group the teens by colors of their bubbles.

Name Tags

Use name tags to create small groups as well as identify the young people. For example, use different-colored or different-shaped name tags for each group. Add colored dots or stickers to the name tags to identify each group. Create more permanent name tags out of leather disks and add different-colored beads to identify the groups. Be creative.

Noah's Ark

Choose one animal to represent each small group. Write the name of each animal on as many slips of paper as you want people in a group. Fold the papers and put them in a basket or a bag. When the young people arrive, instruct them to randomly pick the name of an animal. Tell them not to show anyone else what they chose. When it is time for small groups, direct the teens to imitate the animal they chose. They can make no other sounds but animal sounds during this time, and they are to find others who are imitating the same animal and lock arms with them until the whole group is together.

You can do similar groupings with nursery rhymes, Christmas carols, children's songs, and so forth.

Button Up

Make four signs, each labeled with one of the following headings: "0–3," "4–7," "8–10," and "10+." (You may need to adjust these number spans depending on the size of your group, popular clothing styles, the number of small groups you want to create, and other factors.) Post the signs around the room. When it is time to break into small groups, direct the teens to count the number of buttons visible on the outside of their clothing and stand under the appropriate sign.

Gather By . . .

Use these criteria to creatively gather young teens into small groups:

- eye color
- sock color
- hair color
- number of siblings or people in their immediate family
- number of letters in their first name
- type of pet they own
- favorite subject in school
- preferred soft drink
- odd and even birth months and days
- number of digits in their house number
- only child, youngest child, middle child, oldest child
- shirt or blouse color

Bible Verses

Before the session choose several Bible verses, as many as the number of groups you would like to form. If you are using this as part of a catechetical session, you may want to choose verses that are connected to your lesson. Write each verse in large letters on poster board or newsprint and post the verses around the room. Write the citation for each verse on as many small pieces of paper as you want people in a group. When it is time for small groups, randomly distribute the citations and several Bibles. Tell the young people to look up the citation in the Bible and gather under the correct poster.

Count Off

Counting off is a tried-and-true method of forming groups. Decide on the number of small groups you need. Ask the young teens to count one by one up to that number, starting over from one each time that number is reached. All the ones are in one group, the twos in another, and so forth. For variety, use something other than numbers, such as colors of the rainbow, names of cartoon characters, seasons, names of candy bars, and so forth.

Name Alliteration

Tell the young people to pair up or gather with those whose first name begins with the same letter as their own. If you suspect that the groups will be lopsided because of, for example, a large number of Jasons, Jessicas, and Jareds in attendance, use the first letter of middle names, last names, or nicknames as the organizing criteria.

Forward, March!

This activity works best in a large room. Before the gathering decide how many small groups you need and where they will meet in the room. Designate the meeting spaces by posting a small sign in each space.

Gather all the participants in the center of the room. Tell them that at your signal and at your pace, they are to march forward five (or any number below ten) steps in any direction in the room. Encourage them to cover all parts of the room. Do not tell them that they will ultimately form small groups because if you do, they are more likely to head in the same direction as their friends. Give a signal and start counting the paces. After you reach the number, tell them to gather under the nearest sign. The teens that gather under each sign make up the small group.

It's in the Bag

Put all the young people's names in a paper bag. Randomly pull out the same number of names as you want people in a small group. You might also recruit one or two of the participants to do the drawing. Read each name as it is drawn and direct that person to his or her group's meeting place. Repeat this process for each small group.

NOTES

Use the space below to jot notes and reminders for the next time you use this strategy.

Fifty Ways
to Choose a Leader

Many young teens are reluctant to volunteer for even small leadership roles. Those who are confident, outgoing, popular, and highly social are likely to volunteer all the time, and it is easy for adult leaders to rely on those few to assume leadership roles.

It is important, however, that everyone get a chance to lead at some point, even in a small way. Leading might be as simple as being the first in a group to say something, or collecting supplies for a group project. It might be as involved as being the recorder or the captain of a team during a game. To reduce the level of discomfort that some young teens might feel in the role of leader, the method of choosing a leader must be objective and respectful of young people's emotional safety.

The suggestions for choosing a team leader listed below provide nonthreatening, easy, objective, and fun ways to give everyone the opportunity to be a leader. Many of them also help young people get to know a little more about one another.

1. the person who has visited the most states
2. the person who has the largest immediate family
3. the person who is seated closest to you
4. the person with the most letters in her or his full name
5. the person with the most pets
6. the person who has attended the most professional sports events in the past three months
7. the person who has played a musical instrument longest
8. the person whose birthday is closest to today's date

9. the person with the most buttons visible on her or his clothing
10. the person whose birthday is closest to Christmas
11. the person who has the fewest syllables in her or his full name
12. the person with the oldest sibling
13. the person with the most uncles
14. the person who most recently ate at a fast-food restaurant
15. the person who has been to the dentist or orthodontist most recently
16. the person who gets up earliest for school
17. the person who has the longest bus ride to school
18. the person with the most first cousins
19. the person with the most pieces of jewelry on
20. the person who has had the most broken bones
21. the person who got the least amount of sleep last night
22. the person with the most *M*'s in her or his full name
23. the person who has flown in an airplane the least
24. the person who most recently purchased a CD with her or his own money
25. the person who has lived in the most houses or apartments
26. the person who watched cartoons most recently
27. the person who has the most older siblings
28. the person who watched the least TV in the past week
29. the person who has been shopping most recently
30. the person who has worn braces the longest
31. the person with the youngest sibling
32. the person who lives farthest from the session meeting place
33. the person wearing the most blue
34. the person who has slept in a tent the most times
35. the person who has the most uncles
36. the person who ate the most for breakfast today
37. the person who has been absent from school the fewest days this year
38. the person whose teeth have the most fillings
39. the person with the most grandparents still living
40. the person who has the longest pinkie finger
41. the person who has played on the most organized sports teams
42. the person who plays or has played the most musical instruments
43. the person who spent the least amount of time online in the past week
44. the person with the darkest (or lightest) hair
45. the person who learned to swim at the youngest age
46. the person whose birthday is closest to the leader's
47. the person who has visited the fewest states
48. the person who has been outside the United States most often

49. the person who most recently had to do something in front of a group
50. the person who finished reading a book most recently

NOTES

Use the space below to jot notes and reminders for the next time you use this strategy.

(This strategy is adapted from *Ideas,* no. 40, edited by Wayne Rice and Paul Thigpen, p. 34.)

Part B
Gathering and Mingling

Most young teens have a difficult time mingling with people outside of their immediate circle of friends. This tendency to stay with the people they know best encourages the cliquishness that is prevalent among young adolescents and raises the level of discomfort for those who—by choice or by chance—are not part of a regular group.

The activities in part B provide a safe way for young teens to go beyond their comfort level and move around a group, learn names, and begin conversations. Many of the activities also ease the situation for young people who arrive to a meeting first and are uncomfortable being without their friends or not particularly good at just filling time.

Me Too!

As the young people gather, they list a variety of their preferences. When it is time to mingle, they must find other people who share their preferences.

Suggested Time

About 5 minutes for everyone to complete the preferences handout. Depending on the size of the group, about 10 minutes to find others whose answers match.

Group Size

This activity works best with groups larger than fifteen.

Materials Needed

☼ copies of handout 1, "Me Too!" one for each person
☼ pens or pencils

PROCEDURE

1. Distribute a copy of handout 1, and a pen or a pencil to everyone. An ideal time to do this part of the activity is when the young people arrive at the gathering. Having such a task helps those who are shy or those whose friends have not yet arrived, to avoid feeling awkward or uncomfortable as they wait. Tell the young people to complete the sentences by filling in the blanks on the right side of the handout.

2. Point out that everyone has their own preferences, which is part of what makes us all unique. However, it is likely that people in the room share at least some preferences. Explain that their task is to find as many people as they can who have identified the same preferences as they did. When two people find such a match, they should sign the line to the left of that item on each other's sheets. No one can sign a sheet more than once. Everyone's goal is to fill the left side of the sheet with names of people who share their preferences.

ALTERNATIVE APPROACHES

◎ If you have a group of fewer than fifteen people, you may want to let people sign a sheet more than once.

◎ You may want to offer small prizes to the first three people who get signatures by all the items.

NOTES

Use the space below to jot notes and reminders for the next time you use this strategy.

Me Too!

Complete the sentences below by writing your answers on the blanks to the right. When you are finished, your leader will direct you to find people who have the same preferences as you and have them sign the line to the left of an item that fits them. You cannot have anyone sign this sheet more than once.

_____ 1. My favorite sport to play is _____

_____ 2. My favorite music group is _____

_____ 3. A place I'd like to visit someday is _____

_____ 4. My favorite television show is _____

_____ 5. The saddest movie I ever saw was _____

_____ 6. A chore that I absolutely hate doing is _____ _____

_____ 7. The job I would least like to have is _____

_____ 8. When I'm under stress, I usually _____

_____ 9. When I was five, my favorite television show was _____

_____ 10. My favorite comic strip or cartoon character is _____

_____ 11. A well-known person I admire is _____

_____ 12. My favorite fast-food restaurant is _____

_____ 13. My favorite flavor of ice cream is _____

_____ 14. If I could be famous, I would like to be known for _____

_____ 15. My favorite breakfast cereal is _____

On a Typical Day

OVERVIEW This strategy is a variation of the previous one, but uses a typical daily schedule for the young people to find things in common with one another. This is an especially good activity if the young people in your group go to different schools.

Suggested Time

About 5 minutes for everyone to complete the schedule handout. Depending on the size of the group, about 10 minutes to find others whose answers match.

Group Size

This activity works best with groups larger than fifteen.

Materials Needed

☼ pens or pencils
☼ copies of handout 2, "On a Typical Day," one for each person
☼ a small, inexpensive, fun prize (optional)

PROCEDURE

1. Distribute a pen or a pencil and a copy of handout 2 to everyone. Ask them to think about what they are doing at certain times on a typical school day. For example, they might fill in the 10 a.m. slot with "in math class" or the 4 p.m. slot with "at soccer practice." They should write their usual activity in the line to the right of the time of day. You may need to specify a day of the week because some schools have alternating classes and cocurricular activities are not likely to meet every day.

2. When everyone has completed their sheet, announce that the task is to find other people who are doing the same thing they are at any given time on a typical day. When two people find such a match, they should sign the line to the left of that time on each other's sheets. No one can sign a sheet more than once.
   The first person who fills all her or his lines is the winner. You may want to offer a small, inexpensive, fun prize, such as a toy watch or a used calendar.

ALTERNATIVE APPROACHES

◎ If you have a small group, make up your own sheet with fewer times of the day, or you may want to let people sign two sheets..
◎ If the young people go to the same school, you may want to do the schedule for a Saturday or Sunday instead of a weekday.

NOTES

Use the space below to jot notes and reminders for the next time you use this strategy.

(This strategy is adapted from *Mix It Up!* by Les Christie et al., p. 19.)

On a Typical Day

Complete the statements below by writing your answers on the blanks to the right, based on a typical day in your life. When you are finished, your leader will direct you to find people who are usually doing the same thing you are at a given time and have them sign the line to the left of that time. You cannot have anyone sign this sheet more than once.

_____ At **6 a.m.** I am _____

_____ At **9 a.m.** I am _____

_____ At **11 a.m.** I am _____

_____ At **1 p.m.** I am _____

_____ At **4 p.m.** I am _____

_____ At **6 p.m.** I am _____

_____ At **8 p.m.** I am _____

_____ At **10 p.m.** I am _____

_____ At **midnight** I am _____

Handout 2: Permission to reproduce this handout for program use is granted.

People Bingo

This activity has been around for a long time, but it is still one of the best ways to begin a process of getting to know people. The goal is to fill in each square on a special bingo card with the signature of a different person who fits the description in that square.

Suggested Time

5 to 10 minutes, depending on the size of the group

Group Size

This activity works best with groups of at least twenty people.

Materials Needed

- ☼ pens or pencils
- ☼ copies of handout 3, "People Bingo," one for each person
- ☼ small prizes (optional)

PROCEDURE

Distribute a pen or a pencil and a copy of handout 3 to everyone. Tell them that they are to find a different person in the room who fits the description in each square and get that person to sign the corresponding square. They cannot have anyone sign more than one square.

The first person to get all their squares signed is the winner. You may want to award small or humorous prizes to the first few people who complete the handout.

ALTERNATIVE APPROACHES

◎ If your group is small, you may want to let people sign each sheet twice.
◎ Create your own bingo game. Draw a grid and fill in each box with a characteristic that young teens in your group likely possess or an experience that young teens in your group likely have had.

NOTES

Use the space below to jot notes and reminders for the next time you use this strategy.

People Bingo

Find people who fit the descriptions in the squares. When you find a match, have that person sign the appropriate square. You cannot have anyone sign this sheet more than once.

was born outside of this state	knows how to count to ten in two foreign languages	never owned a Barbie doll	read a book in the last seven days	ate at a fast-food restaurant in the last seven days
takes (or has taken) music lessons	plays a competitive sport	has had a broken limb	has brothers	owns a recording of classical music
is at least five years older or younger than you	is the oldest child in the family	likes the same television shows you do	is a morning person	is artistic
has visited a foreign country	saw a movie in a movie theater in the last seven days	has money in a pocket or purse	did not watch *Sesame Street* as a child	walks or bikes to school or work
is good at math	will spend part of the summer away from home	can ice skate	earns money at a job (allowance not included)	has seen or talked with a grandparent in the last seven days

Junk Mixer

OVERVIEW

This is a good exercise for learning names. Each young person is given a household item to wear and a list of the items everyone is wearing. The task is to find out the name of each person and write it on the list next to the item that person is wearing.

Suggested Time

5 to 10 minutes, depending on the size of the group

Group Size

This activity works best with groups of fifteen to thirty-five. If your group is larger or smaller, see the alternative approaches for ways to adapt the activity.

Materials Needed

- an assortment of common household or office items (such as a rubber band, a spoon, a craft stick, a pencil, a button, a battery, a paper clip, and a sandwich bag), one item for each person
- materials to fasten or attach the items to the participants or their clothing, such as masking tape, string, rubber bands, straight pins, and safety pins
- copies of a master list of the items, one for each person
- pens or pencils
- a few small prizes or certificates of award (optional)

PROCEDURE

Preparation. Make a master list of all the household or office items that you will be using in this activity. Next to each item, add a line long enough for a name. Make one copy of the master list for each participant.

Place in a central location in the gathering space the fastening materials that you gathered.

1. As the young people arrive, give each of them one of the household or office items that you collected. Point out the fastening materials, and tell the young teens that they must attach the item to their person or their clothing. The item should be clearly visible, but it does not have to be in an obvious location. For example, they might pin a paper clip to their shirtsleeve or tape a button to the top of a shoe.

2. Distribute copies of the master list and a pen or a pencil to each person. Tell them that they must find the person who is wearing each item on the list and write his or her name next to that item. Explain that no one can announce or otherwise point out what they or another person is wearing. They must leave it to others to find the items for themselves.

The first person to complete the list is the winner. You may want to award a small prize or a certificate that says, "Expert junk collector," to the first few people to finish their list.

ALTERNATIVE APPROACHES

◎ If you have more than thirty-five participants, you may want to divide the group up and give each smaller group a different master list. For example, if you have fifty young teens in your group, you may want to put twenty-five items on one list and give it to one half of the group, and put twenty-five items on another list and give it to the other half of the group.

◎ If you have a small group, give each person several items to attach. Place the items in an envelope and separate the young people so that they can attach the items without being observed. By doing this no one else knows what items the others have or where they have attached them.

◎ Instead of doing this activity all at once, give the young people a few minutes periodically throughout the session to complete the list. This method gives the young people several breaks to move around and also to meet new people.

NOTES

Use the space below to jot notes and reminders for the next time you use this strategy.

(This strategy is adapted from *First Impressions,* compiled by Pamela J. Shoup, p. 72.)

The Week in Review

OVERVIEW The young teens find out how much they have in common with one another, by signing their name to various experiences and characteristics posted on a wall. This activity works well during a gathering time and helps young people see that they are not alone in their experiences or personal characteristics.

Suggested Time

About 10 minutes, depending on the size of the group

Group Size

This activity works with any size group.

Materials Needed

- ☼ pens or pencils
- ☼ sheets of 8½-by-11-inch paper, ten or more
- ☼ a marker
- ☼ masking tape
- ☼ a step stool (optional)

PROCEDURE

Preparation. At the top of each of several sheets of paper, write an experience that the young people may have had this week. Leave room underneath the statement for signatures. Make at least nine signs, enough to create a bingo-style grid. Put a different experience on each sheet. A few sample experiences follow:

◎ walked or rode a bike around the lake
◎ watched a football game
◎ got at least a B on an assignment or a test
◎ ate fast food
◎ argued with someone
◎ did something with the family
◎ earned money
◎ read from a book or magazine for pleasure
◎ competed against someone for something
◎ greeted or smiled at a stranger

Post the signs on an empty wall in a grid, like the squares of a bingo card. Above the grid place a sign that reads, "The week in review."

1. As the participants arrive, give them each a pen or a pencil and tell them to sign their name to any of the sheets posted on the wall that apply to them. You may want to provide a step stool to help the shorter members of the group reach the top items.

2. Comment on the results, noting things such as the following:

◎ the item that got the most signatures
◎ the item that got the fewest signatures or none at all
◎ the number of things people have in common, and the likelihood that no matter what we experience, we are not alone
◎ the uniqueness of people's choices, and the likelihood that no matter how much we have in common, we will always have things that set us apart from one another

ALTERNATIVE APPROACH

◎ Instead of reviewing the week, make the activity knowledge-based by writing items like, "Can name the seven sacraments" and "Knows the names of the four Gospel writers." Title your grid accordingly, for example, "Bible bingo."

NOTES

Use the space below to jot notes and reminders for the next time you use this strategy.

In-Place Scavenger Hunt

The young teens work in small groups to find specific items that they have in their pockets or backpack, or on their person, and are awarded points for those items. The small groups compete for the highest point total. This activity builds a sense of unity and common purpose among group members.

Suggested Time

About 10 minutes

Group Size

This activity works with any number of participants. Small groups should have no more than ten people, including the facilitator.

Materials Needed

- ☼ copies of resource 3, "Scavenger Hunt," one for each small-group leader
- ☼ pens or pencils
- ☼ one or more calculators (optional)
- ☼ small prizes (optional)

PROCEDURE

1. Designate someone in each small group as the leader. Suggestions for naming a leader in an objective and nonthreatening way can be found in the activity "Fifty Ways to Choose a Leader" on pages 48–50. Give each small-group leader a copy of resource 3 and a pen or a pencil.

2. Explain to the participants that their task is to find as many examples of the items on the list as they can, using only their pockets, their backpack, or their person as sources. They cannot move to other parts of the room to find the examples, and they may not consult with people from other small groups. The small-group leaders will each keep track of the number of examples their group finds and calculate the point totals. You may want to provide them with calculators. Set a time limit of 5 to 10 minutes.

3. When time is up, collect the sheets and name the winning group. You may want to provide small prizes. You could also name the groups that had the most points on particular items and award prizes to them, so that in the end, everyone gets a prize.

ALTERNATIVE APPROACH

◎ If your group is small, do this activity in pairs or individually. If you do it with individuals, read the list aloud afterward, and compare totals on each item as you go through the list.

NOTES

Use the space below to jot notes and reminders for the next time you use this strategy.

Scavenger Hunt

Read each item on the list and ask the members of your group to find examples of that item on their person or in their belongings. Multiply the number of points allotted to that item by the number of examples of that item the group holds. Then add the total points for items 1 to 20 to get the total points for the group.

Item	Number of that item x points per example of that item = total points per item
1. photos of family members (5 points)	_____ x 5 = _____
2. buttons on clothing (2 points)	_____ x 2 = _____
3. pens and pencils (3 points)	_____ x 3 = _____
4. rings and earrings (5 points)	_____ x 5 = _____
5. belts (10 points)	_____ x 10 = _____
6. eyeglasses and sunglasses (20 points)	_____ x 20 = _____
7. something with the name of a local school on it (10 points)	_____ x 10 = _____
8. something with the name or logo of a professional sports team on it (5 points)	_____ x 5 = _____
9. shoelaces (7 points)	_____ x 7 = _____
10. zippers (10 points)	_____ x 10 = _____
11. pieces of gum (8 points)	_____ x 8 = _____
12. combs or brushes (4 points)	_____ x 4 = _____
13. socks (10 points)	_____ x 10 = _____
14. holes in socks (20 points)	_____ x 20 = _____
15. religious items (25 points)	_____ x 25 = _____
16. electronic items (10 points)	_____ x 10 = _____
17. coins (5 points)	_____ x 5 = _____
18. keys (7 points)	_____ x 7 = _____
19. sets of braces (10 points)	_____ x 10 = _____
20. watches (7 points)	_____ x 7 = _____

Total points for the group _____

Collage Name Tags

The young people make name tags that identify them not only by name but also by character, preferences, gifts, and so forth. This activity helps young teens articulate who they are and who they want to become.

Suggested Time

At least 15 minutes, but the activity can go on for much longer

Group Size

This activity works with any size group, as long as you have enough materials for everyone and a few adults to help monitor the group.

Materials Needed

- scissors, one for each person
- glue sticks, one for each person
- 2-by-3-inch plastic name badges with paper inserts, one for each person
- a variety of catalogs, magazines, newspaper inserts, and so forth

PROCEDURE

1. Give each person a scissors, a glue stick, and a plastic name badge with a paper insert. Distribute a variety of catalogs, magazines, newspaper inserts, and so on. Tell the young people to create minicollage name tags using small pictures and words from the print materials. The completed name tags should tell a variety of things about them: things they like, things they are good at, things that are important to them, and so forth. On the top of the collage, they are to paste the letters of their name, which they must also cut out of the print materials.

You may want to set a minimum number of items that must appear on the tag, or you may require that the entire front of the insert be covered with small pictures and words. Encourage the young people to ask one another to look for specific items or words. Keep close track of the time and announce when it is running out.

2. Ask the young people to share their name tag with their group, explaining what it says about who they are. Allow other members of the group to examine the name tag closely and ask questions of the owner.

ALTERNATIVE APPROACHES

◎ Consider focusing the theme by doing blessing name tags, gift name tags, dream name tags, and so forth.

◎ On the back of the name tags, tell the young people to paste pictures and words that tell about the things that they do not always reveal to others. Those might include their fears, their aspirations, things that make them cry, and things that make them angry.

◎ Instead of name tags, have the young people make collage bookmarks or miniposters. If possible, laminate their creations. Suggest that the young teens use the bookmark in their Bible or a schoolbook, or hang the poster in their locker, to remind them of God's presence.

NOTES

Use the space below to jot notes and reminders for the next time you use this strategy.

Name-Tag Autographs

OVERVIEW

The young people circulate among the group first to find the owner of a name tag, and second to gather as many autographs as possible in the allotted time.

Suggested Time

10 to 15 minutes

Group Size

This activity works best with groups of fifteen to fifty people.

Materials Needed

- 5-by-8-inch index cards, one for each person
- a marker
- a paper punch
- string or yarn
- pens or pencils
- a small prize (optional)

PROCEDURE

Preparation. Write each person's name on a 5-by-8-inch index card. Punch two holes above each name and attach string or yarn so that the name tag can be worn around the neck.

1. Randomly distribute (insofar as ensuring that no one gets their own name) the name tags to the participants, along with pens or pencils. Tell them that they are to find the owner of the name tag and give it to that person.

2. After the participants have given the name tag to its owner and received their own name tag, they are to mingle with other people and gather autographs on their name tag. Before they ask someone for their autograph, they must find out a little-known fact about that person. Some examples follow:
◎ the state the person was born in
◎ a favorite season
◎ a favorite time of day
◎ what the person usually has for breakfast
◎ a parent's line of work or profession

Set a time limit for exchanging name tags and gathering autographs and information. Announce when the time limit is approaching.

3. Gather all the participants in the meeting space. Ask them to count the number of autographs they received. You may want to award a small prize to the person who gathered the most signatures.

As time allows, ask the young people to share some of the little-known facts they found out about one another.

NOTES

Use the space below to jot notes and reminders for the next time you use this strategy.

(This strategy is adapted from *Creative Crowd-Breakers, Mixers, and Games,* compiled by Wayne Rice and Mike Yaconelli, p. 30.)

Things in Common

OVERVIEW

The participants work in small groups to find ten things that all group members have in common. This is a good activity for helping young teens realize that they are not alone in their experiences or preferences.

Suggested Time

About 15 minutes

Group Size

This activity works with any size group.

Materials Needed

- ☼ newsprint, one sheet for each small group
- ☼ markers, one for each small group
- ☼ masking tape

PROCEDURE

1. Divide the participants into small groups using one of the grouping activities in part A of this book. For the sake of comfort among the young teens, each group should consist of at least six people.

2. Give each small group a sheet of newsprint and a marker. Designate someone in each group as the recorder. Tell the groups that they are each to come up with ten things that all the small-group members have in common and write them on the newsprint. Stress that they should avoid obvious commonalities, such as "We're all human" or "We're all in the seventh grade." Encourage them instead to find experiences and preferences that they all share. Give examples like the following:

◎ We've all seen the movie _____ [name a current movie].
◎ We were all born in a different state.
◎ We all wear glasses or contacts.
◎ We all learned to Rollerblade in the second grade.
◎ We are all the oldest child in the family.

3. When the groups have completed their task, ask them to read their list for the rest of the participants. Post the lists in a conspicuous place.
Conclude with comments along the following lines:

Although we tend to focus on the things that make us different from one another, we have far more in common than we think we do. One way to build mutual trust and respect is to concentrate on the things we have in common. Only then can we appreciate the things that make us different and unique in all the world.

ALTERNATIVE APPROACHES

◎ To extend this activity or to broaden the focus, have each person come up with something that makes her or him unique from others in the group. Suggest things like "I like to go fly fishing with my dad" or "My grandparents were born in another country" or "I play the cello." If you do not have time to extend the activity, but you still want to use this alternative, shorten step 2 by having the small groups find only five things in common.
◎ Compare all the lists to see if any experiences or preferences listed are common to the entire group.

NOTES

Use the space below to jot notes and reminders for the next time you use this strategy.

ID Cup

The participants decorate disposable cups with identifying words and phrases and share the information with one another.

Suggested Time

About 10 minutes

Group Size

This activity works with any size group.

Materials Needed

- ☼ clear or light-colored disposable drinking cups, one for each person
- ☼ thin-line permanent markers, one for each person
- ☼ newsprint and markers
- ☼ masking tape

PROCEDURE

Preparation. Write the following sentence-starters on newsprint and post the newsprint in a conspicuous place:

◎ My name is . . .
◎ Something I like to do is . . .
◎ Something I'm good at is . . .
◎ My friends think I . . .
◎ In twenty years I hope that I . . .
◎ Something I've never done that I'd like to do someday is . . .
◎ I am . . .
◎ I wish . . .

1. Give the participants each a disposable cup and a permanent marker. Call their attention to the sentence-starters on the newsprint that you posted. Tell them to write their name in an obvious location on the cup and then to write answers to the sentence-starters on the cup. Caution everyone to wait until the ink dries before they handle their cup.

2. Ask for volunteers to share their answers to certain sentence-starters. When it is time for refreshments, suggest that people mingle and read one another's cups.

ALTERNATIVE APPROACHES

◎ Suggest that the participants decorate their disposable cup. Make available a variety of colors of permanent markers, stickers, magazines, scissors, glue sticks, and so forth.
◎ Purchase more-permanent drinking vessels, such as plastic picnic cups. Have the young teens decorate their cup at the first session of the year or at the beginning of a retreat. Use these cups for refreshments throughout the year or the event.

NOTES

Use the space below to jot notes and reminders for the next time you use this strategy.

Number, Please

| OVERVIEW |

This strategy uses a deck of cards to help the young people get to know a little more about one another. Everyone responds to a topic dictated by the number of the card they are dealt.

Suggested Time

About 10 minutes, depending on the number of rounds and the number of people in a small group

Group Size

This activity works with any size group.

Materials Needed

- ☼ decks of cards, one for each small group
- ☼ copies of resource 4, "Number, Please," one for each small group

PROCEDURE

Gather the participants into small groups of four to seven people each. Designate someone in each group to be a leader. Give each leader a deck of cards with the face cards and jokers removed, and a copy of resource 4. Tell the leader to deal the cards one by one to the group members, including himself or herself, waiting after each card for the recipient to address the topic on the "Number, Please" sheet that corresponds to the number of the card. Assure everyone that they do not have to give lengthy answers. Let the leaders continue dealing in this manner for as long as you like.

ALTERNATIVE APPROACHES

- After the young people get through a few rounds of cards, distribute notebook paper and pens or pencils. Tell everyone to write down as much as they remember about what the person to their right said.
- To speed up this activity, use only the cards from ace to five, and only items 1 to 5 on resource 4.
- Change this activity into a learning or review activity by tailoring the topics to the things you are studying. For example:
  1. Name *one* miracle of Jesus.
  2. Name *two* books in the New Testament.
  3. Name *three* Apostles of Jesus.

NOTES

Use the space below to jot notes and reminders for the next time you use this strategy.

Number, Please

1. If you could change *one* thing about the world, what would it be?

2. What *two* personal achievements are you proud of?

3. What are *three* things that make you laugh?

4. Name *four* things you do before you go to school in the morning.

5. What are your *five* top movies of all time?

6. What were your *six* favorite toys when you were a child?

7. Name *seven* things you ate or drank today.

8. What was your favorite television show when you were *eight*?

9. What are you usually doing at *nine* o'clock in the evening?

10. What is one thing you think you'll be doing *ten* years from now?

Expectations Autographs

All families have rules and expectations. This activity allows the young teens to share with their peers some of their responsibilities at home and other expectations of their parents. It is a good way to begin a session on family relationships, rights and responsibilities, or maturity.

Suggested Time

About 10 minutes

Group Size

This activity works with any size group.

Materials Needed

- ☼ copies of handout 4, "Expectations Autographs," one for each person
- ☼ pens or pencils

PROCEDURE

Distribute to each person a copy of handout 4 and a pen or a pencil. Tell everyone that they are to find different people in the room whose families expect them to carry out the tasks and responsibilities on the handout, and get those persons each to sign to the right of the item that applies to them. Point out that they cannot have anyone sign their paper more than once.

ALTERNATIVE APPROACHES

◎ Post a sheet of newsprint and provide markers. Ask the young teens to write on the newsprint any family expectations that are not on the handout. When someone adds an item, others can sign their name to it if it pertains to them.

◎ Instead of distributing the handout, copy the expectations each on a separate sheet of paper and post them on a wall. Tell the young teens to sign the expectations and responsibilities that pertain to them. This method allows them to see that they are not the only ones whose parents expect certain things from them. It is a good way to engage young teens while they are waiting for an event or meeting to begin or during break times. It also works well for a small group.

NOTES

Use the space below to jot notes and reminders for the next time you use this strategy.

(This strategy is adapted from *First Impressions,* compiled by Pamela J. Shoup, pp. 66–67 and 68.)

Expectations Autographs

Find people who have the following responsibilities and expectations at home, and have them sign the line next to a task or role that fits them. You may not have anyone sign this sheet more than once.

At home, I am expected to . . .

☀ take care of a pet   _____

☀ keep my room clean   _____

☀ go to church every weekend   _____

☀ baby-sit my sibling(s)   _____

☀ get grades of 85 percent (B) or higher on   _____
  my report cards

☀ do the dishes   _____

☀ work for my allowance   _____

☀ help with yard work or housework   _____

☀ earn my own spending money working for   _____
  other people

☀ save part of the money I earn or receive as _____
  a gift

☀ make my lunch   _____

☀ keep a curfew   _____

☀ do my homework before I watch TV or get on _____
  the computer

☀ stay home on school nights   _____

☀ limit the time I spend on the telephone, at   _____
  the computer, or watching television

Handout 4: Permission to reproduce this handout for program use is granted.

Crazy Crossing

This strategy is an active way for young teens to find out a little more about one another and mix the group up in the process. It is a good way to start a meeting or to add an energetic mixer to a retreat or longer session. It is best done in a large area without too many obstructions.

Suggested Time

5 to 15 minutes, depending on how many phrases you use

Group Size

This activity works best with groups of more than ten people.

PROCEDURE

1. Divide the participants into two teams. Have the teams line up against a wall on opposite sides of the room. Tell the young people that you will read a number of phrases. If a phrase applies to them, they must switch sides.

2. Read phrases from the following list or make up your own. Keep them brief and occasionally call out a phrase that applies to everyone. Continue until the teams are well mixed.

- I'm wearing socks.
- My shoes are untied.
- I'm wearing something blue.
- I got an A on a test this week.
- I am the youngest in my family.
- I like broccoli.
- I was not born in this state.
- I am an only child.
- I like to spend time on the computer.
- I play a musical instrument.
- I play an organized sport.
- I've already finished my homework for the next school day.
- I earn money (other than an allowance from parents).
- I have my own room.
- At least one grandparent lives in the same town I do.
- I think I know what I want to be when I grow up.
- I like to read.
- I like to go camping.
- I can cook breakfast for myself.
- My favorite season is summer.

ALTERNATIVE APPROACH

- You may want to explore some of the answers. For example, ask those who said they are the youngest in the family, "What do you see as the advantages and disadvantages of the situation?" For those who like to read, ask, "What was the last book you read or the best book you read in the last year?"

NOTES

Use the space below to jot notes and reminders for the next time you use this strategy.

(This strategy is adapted from *Growing Close,* edited by Stephen Parolini, p. 24.)

Short Activities
for Waiting Times

OVERVIEW

Young teens are frequently uncomfortable when they are alone with an adult whom they do no know well or in the company of peers who are not close friends. The activities in this section are useful for times such as these:

- before the start of a class or an activity
- during snack breaks or mealtimes on a retreat
- when waiting for other people or groups to finish a project
- during free time in an extended session

Suggested Time

Most of these activities do not need to be done all at once and can be done over a period of time. This allows the young people the freedom to come back to a task when they need to and you, as the leader, the flexibility to move on with your plan for the class or session when you need to.

Group Size

These activities work with any size group.

Materials Needed

Many of the activities in this section require nothing more than you would normally have available for a gathering of young teens: pens or pencils, markers, newsprint, and so forth. For activities that rely on handouts, those are provided at the end of the section.

SUGGESTED STRATEGIES

Group Puzzle

If your group usually meets in the same location and you have space available, make a jigsaw puzzle available for young teens who arrive early or for break times. Encourage all the participants to get involved in the puzzle. You can use it to teach about perseverance, patience, God-given talents, creativity, trial and error, and so forth.

Crossword Challenge

Use a photocopier to enlarge a crossword puzzle that is appropriate for young teens. Post the puzzle on the wall along with its clues. Make pencils available and challenge the participants to complete the puzzle. You can make this a small-group competition by enlarging several puzzles and assigning one to each small group.

Candy Count

Empty a bag or two of small candies, such as M&M's or Skittles, into a clear glass or plastic bowl. Invite the participants to guess the number of candies in the bowl. Provide small pieces of paper and pencils so that the young people can write their name and their number estimate. When the time comes to announce a winner, admit that you have no idea how many candies are in the bowl, and share the candy with everyone. The young teens may complain, but the activity will have served its purpose: to engage them in a neutral activity and help lessen the anxiety that may affect some people.

Graffiti Wall

Post several sheets of newsprint on a wall and supply a variety of markers. Provide a sentence-starter that is related to your theme for the day. For example, if you are doing a session on prayer, you could write the phrase, "Prayer is . . . ," at the top of the newsprint. If you are doing a class on discipleship, you might write, "To be a Christian means . . ." Encourage the young people to finish the sentence with their own thoughts. They might also add drawings, pictures, and messages to the wall, as time allows.

Word Puzzles

Many young teens, with their developing sense of logic and ability to see beyond the obvious, enjoy the challenge of word puzzles, also known as rebuses and wuzzles. Make copies of handout 5, "Word Puzzles," available for their use. You can also copy each puzzle onto a separate sheet of paper, post all the puzzles on a wall, and ask the young teens to work together to figure out their meaning. The answers follow:

1. spreading the Gospel
2. upper room
3. frankincense
4. mixed messages
5. too much of a good thing
6. not enough money to cover the check
7. stretching the truth
8. smokestack
9. three-piece suit
10. eggs over easy
11. fly in the ointment
12. sign on the dotted line
13. sideshow
14. pie in the sky
15. feeling under the weather
16. splitting the difference
17. fancy footwork
18. to be or not to be
19. bouncing baby boy
20. slanting the news
21. condensed books
22. It's a small world.
23. skinny-dipping
24. A bird in the hand equals two in the bush.
25. scrambled eggs
26. That's beside the point.
27. hanging in there
28. flat tire

Food Foibles

Provide everyone with a copy of handout 6, "Food Foibles." Tell them that each numbered item is the list of the ingredients in a popular food or snack item. Their task is to figure out what item is represented by each list of ingredients. The answers follow:

1. bubblegum
2. corn chips
3. pasta
4. pretzels
5. raisin bran cereal
6. cola

7. peanut butter
8. vanilla ice cream
9. chocolate chip cookies
10. Popsicles

Pigskin Puzzlers

Distribute to everyone a copy of handout 7, "Pigskin Puzzlers." Explain that each phrase represents one team from the National Football League. Their task is to determine what the real name of the team is. The answers to the quiz follow:

1. Tennessee Titans
2. San Francisco 49ers
3. Tampa Bay Buccaneers
4. Saint Louis Rams
5. Buffalo Bills
6. Denver Broncos
7. Carolina Panthers
8. Green Bay Packers
9. Dallas Cowboys
10. Kansas City Chiefs
11. New Orleans Saints
12. Detroit Lions
13. Minnesota Vikings
14. Philadelphia Eagles
15. Arizona Cardinals
16. Indianapolis Colts
17. Seattle Seahawks
18. Pittsburgh Steelers
19. New York Giants
20. Miami Dolphins
21. Baltimore Ravens
22. Washington Redskins
23. Atlanta Falcons
24. New York Jets
25. San Diego Chargers
26. Chicago Bears
27. Cincinnati Bengals
28. Oakland Raiders
29. Jacksonville Jaguars
30. Cleveland Browns
31. New England Patriots

(This strategy is adapted from *Ideas,* nos. 49–52, edited by Wayne Rice and Tim McLaughlin, pp. 48–49.)

ALTERNATIVE APPROACHES

◎ The handout activities in this section can be turned into group projects by copying the contents of the handout onto a large sheet of paper and posting it on the wall. People can work together to find the answer or solve the problem.

◎ Use the activities that require problem-solving abilities as group projects when small groups are in their early stages of forming. Such team projects can build a sense of group cohesiveness.

◎ Ask for volunteers to create sports quizzes along the lines of Pigskin Puzzlers for the National Basketball Association, the National Hockey League, and major league baseball.

NOTES

Use the space below to jot notes and reminders for the next time you use this strategy.

Word Puzzles

Each of the following puzzles depicts a common word or phrase. For example:

TAKE
TAKE = double take   or $\dfrac{\text{STAND}}{\text{I}}$ = I understand.

Your task is to decide what word or phrase each puzzle depicts.

1 G　o　s　p　e　l	2 room	3 **CENFRANKSE**	4 emseassg megassse samegess gemasses measegss
5　a good thing a good 　thing a good thing a 　good thing a good thing a good thing a good thing a good thing a good thing a good thing a good thing a good thing a good thing	6 **MONE**✓	7 **truth**	8 smoke smoke smoke smoke smoke smoke smoke
9 **S UI T**	10 **EGGS** **EASY**	11 **OINTFLYMENT**	12 ....**SIGN**............
13 ЅHOW	14 **SPIEKY**	15 THE WEATHER FEELING	16 **differ ence**
17 *footwork*	18 **BBORNOTBB**	19 baby boy	20 *NEWS*
21 **BOOKS**	22 world	23 D I P P I N G	24 **HABIRDND = BUTWOSH**
25 geεb	26 T H A T 'S　•	27 IN THERE	28 **TIRE**

Handout 5: Permission to reproduce this handout for program use is granted.

Food Foibles

Each list of ingredients below makes up a popular food or snack item. Read each list and guess what item is being described.

_____ 1. sugar, dextrose, corn syrup (glucose), gum base, high fructose corn syrup, corn starch, artificial flavor and color (including FDGG red 3), BHT (to maintain freshness)

_____ 2. corn, vegetable oil (contains one or more of the following: corn, sunflower, or partially hydrogenated sunflower oil), and salt

_____ 3. semolina, enriched with iron (ferrous sulfate), and B vitamins (niacin, thiamine mononitrate, riboflavin, folic acid).

_____ 4. soft red wheat flour, corn syrup, salt, vegetable oil (soybean), sodium bicarbonate, yeast

_____ 5. whole grain wheat, raisins, wheat bran, sugar, corn syrup, salt, wheat flour, malted barley flour, honey

_____ 6. carbonated water, high fructose corn syrup and/or sucrose, caramel color, phosphoric acid, natural flavors, caffeine

_____ 7. roasted peanuts, sugar, partially hydrogenated vegetable oils

_____ 8. milk, cream, skim milk, sugar, egg yolks, natural flavor, carob bean gum, guar gum, carrageenan, dextrose

_____ 9. enriched flour, vegetable shortening, sugar, semisweet chocolate, salt, sodium bicarbonate, eggs, natural and artificial flavors, emulsifiers

_____ 10. water, high fructose corn syrup, corn syrup, sugar, citric acid, flavoring (water, natural and artificial flavor, modified food starch, citric acid, red 40, yellow 6, blue 1, caramel color, red 3, sodium benzoate as preservative), guar gum, dextrose, karaya gum.

Pigskin Puzzlers

Each phrase below represents one team in the National Football League. Write the real name of the team on the line next to the clue.

_____ 1. Greek giants

_____ 2. gold rushers

_____ 3. pirates

_____ 4. horn bashers

_____ 5. monthly debts

_____ 6. rodeo mounts

_____ 7. big black cats

_____ 8. suitcase stuffers

_____ 9. ropin' ranch hands

_____ 10. Indian leaders

_____ 11. holy people

_____ 12. jungle kings

_____ 13. Scandinavian explorers

_____ 14. bald birds

_____ 15. red birds

_____ 16. baby horses

_____ 17. bay birds

_____ 18. iron men

_____ 19. Jolly Green's cousins

_____ 20. Flipper's friends

_____ 21. shiny black birds

_____ 22. Spiderman's body covers

_____ 23. trained hunting hawks

_____ 24. flying machines

_____ 25. battery boosters

_____ 26. teddies and grizzlies

_____ 27. Indian tigers

_____ 28. refrigerator thieves

_____ 29. spotted cats

_____ 30. brunettes

_____ 31. Revolutionary heroes

Part C
Getting to Know One Another

A community is a group of people who first know about one another, then get to know one another in a deeper way, and finally come together for a common purpose. The strategies in this section help young teens accomplish the second task: getting to know one another.

Most young adolescents do not yet have the social skills necessary to initiate and carry on a conversation with a person they do not know well. The strategies that follow provide helpful directives, clear limits, and subject matter that will engage the young people at a level that is comfortable for them.

Skittles Starters

The participants use multicolored candies to determine their topics for conversation. This is a good check-in activity for classes or group meetings and a small-group builder for longer sessions. You can use this activity several times in one session, changing the topics each time.

Suggested Time

The length of this activity depends on the number of people in the group and the number of rounds. Two rounds in a group of six people is likely to take about 10 minutes.

Group Size

This strategy works with any size group. However, if you have more than fifteen participants, you may want to form smaller groups.

Materials Needed

- a bowl or bowls, one for each group
- a bag of multicolored candies, such as Skittles, M&M's, or jelly beans
- resource 5, "Conversation-Starters" (optional)
- newsprint and markers
- masking tape

PROCEDURE

Preparation. Empty a bag of multicolored candies into a bowl. If you have more than one group, you will need one bowl for each small group.

For each color of candy, you will need one conversation-starter. You may choose the topics from resource 5 or make up your own. Be sure that your categories can elicit multiple answers from the same person in case someone happens to choose the same color of candy each round. Write the conversation-starters on newsprint and indicate what color of candy is associated with each one. Post the list.

1. Put a bowl of multicolored candy in the middle of the group. Point out the list you posted and explain that in turn each person will pick a candy from the bowl and talk about the topic associated with the color he or she chose.

2. Ask for a volunteer to start, or choose a person at random. Hold the bowl above eye level for the first person while he or she randomly chooses a candy. Encourage the young people to listen carefully to one another and not get distracted. Be sure to include yourself in the conversation.

Go through as many rounds of conversation-starters as you have time for or the young teens have interest in.

ALTERNATIVE APPROACHES

◎ Any object that comes in multiple forms can be used for this activity. For example, you could use animal crackers and associate each animal with a category. Use all the pieces of Alpha-Bits cereal that spell out the name of your group or church, and associate each letter with a category. Or use nonfood items such as marbles, Lego bricks, or small squares of colored paper.

◎ Use this as a learning or review activity by changing the categories so that they cover the material. For example, if you are teaching a group about the New Testament, you might see how much they already know by choosing topics such as these:
  ◎ red: something about the Gospel writers
  ◎ yellow: something about the friends of Jesus
  ◎ green: something about the New Testament letters
  ◎ orange: something about the parables of Jesus
  ◎ purple: something about the miracles of Jesus

◎ You may want to end the activity by having everyone take a turn choosing the category that they want to address.

NOTES

Use the space below to jot notes and reminders for the next time you use this strategy.

Conversation-Starters

66 something about your family 99

66 something that is a favorite of yours 99

66 something about school 99

66 something your friends would say about you 99

66 a hobby, or something you do outside of school 99

66 a question you've always wondered about 99

66 something that is a least favorite of yours 99

66 something that makes you angry 99

66 something you would like to ask God 99

66 something you haven't done that you would like to do someday 99

66 a place you would like to visit someday 99

66 someone you know whom you really admire 99

66 something that caused you stress recently 99

66 something that makes you laugh 99

66 a historical person you would like to have known 99

66 something your family likes to do together 99

66 something that worried you recently 99

66 a good thing that happened to you recently 99

66 a not-so-good thing that happened to you recently 99

66 something you hope to own in twenty years 99

66 something you hope to be doing in twenty years 99

66 a nice thing that someone did for you recently 99

66 a nice thing that you did for someone else recently 99

66 something that makes you happy 99

66 a tradition in your family 99

The Doors of Our Lives

This get-to-know-you activity uses a door motif to help the young teens get in touch with their openness to relationships. It is ideal for small groups in a retreat setting, for an opening activity in a meeting on friendship, or to extend a class session.

Suggested Time

About 10 minutes

Group Size

This activity works with any size group. If you have more than ten participants, form smaller groups.

Special Considerations

This activity requires some abstract thinking. Most young adolescents in sixth, seventh, or eighth grade will have no problem with this exercise. However, some younger participants who have not demonstrated an appropriate capacity for conceptualizing may have difficulty understanding the connections between doors and self-awareness.

Materials Needed

- ☼ newsprint and markers
- ☼ masking tape

PROCEDURE

Preparation. List the following types of doors on a sheet of newsprint. Leave space for other types of doors that the young people may add to the list.

◎ revolving door
◎ screen door
◎ sliding glass door
◎ storm door
◎ double doors
◎ pet door
◎ automatic door

1. Display the newsprint list of doors that you prepared. Note that each door represents a way in which people approach relationships. Explain the symbolism of each type of door in the following manner:

If I'm a *revolving door,* I let people in and out of my life on a regular basis.

If I'm a *screen door,* I carefully screen the people whom I allow to enter my life.

If I'm a *sliding glass door,* people can look in on my life but cannot always enter it.

If I'm a *storm door,* I keep people out until the "storm" is over.

If I'm *double doors,* I let lots of people into my life.

If I'm a *pet door,* I'm always open, day or night.

If I'm an *automatic door,* I make it easy for people to come inside and get to know me.

2. Ask the young people if they would add any other types of doors to the list. For example, they might mention garage door, car door, or refrigerator door. Be sure that they explain how the door they name applies to relationships. Add their ideas to the list.

3. Invite the young people to tell the group which door best represents their approach to relationships. To conclude the exercise, make a few brief comments to connect the exercise with the rest of the material you are covering. For example, you might comment on the following points:

◎ the value of knowing how one handles relationships
◎ the importance of being open to new relationships
◎ the circumstances that could change the type of door that represents a person

ALTERNATIVE APPROACHES

◎ Instead of displaying a list of doors on newsprint, find pictures of different kinds of doors in magazines. Mount each picture on a piece of poster board. As you describe the characteristic of each type of door, show the corresponding picture.

◎ If you have time, give the young people a variety of magazines and have them find pictures of doors.

◎ Allow the young people to brainstorm the entire list of doors and what they represent.

◎ If the young people do not know one another well, consider asking them to write about or draw the type of door that represents their approach to new relationships. Keep the exercise anonymous.

SCRIPTURAL CONNECTIONS

Begin or conclude the exercise by reading aloud one or both of the following scriptural passages:

◎ Luke 11:9–10 (Knock and the door will be opened.)

◎ Rev. 3:20 (God is knocking at the door.)

NOTES

Use the space below to jot notes and reminders for the next time you use this strategy.

Blessing Banners

OVERVIEW The young teens think of blessings in their life based on the letters in their name. Those blessings are made into large name tags. This is a good gathering activity for a retreat or as an introduction to a session on identity.

Suggested Time

About 10 minutes

Group Size

This strategy works with any size group.

Materials Needed

- ☼ sheets of construction paper or poster board, about 9-by-12 inches, one for each person
- ☼ markers
- ☼ a hole punch
- ☼ string or yarn

PROCEDURE

1. Give each person a sheet of construction paper or poster board and a variety of markers. Tell everyone to write their first name in large letters down the left side of the paper. For every letter of their name, they are to come up with a blessing in their life that starts with that letter. For example:

Music
Ability to teach
Relationships
Intelligence
Love for my work
Youth ministry
Nieces, nephews, and the rest of my family

2. Make available a hole punch and pieces of string or yarn. When the young people finish their banner, they can punch two holes in the top, put a string through it, and hang it around their neck. If time allows, invite them to share their blessings with the group and offer explanations and clarifications where necessary.

ALTERNATIVE APPROACHES

◎ Purchase plain white t-shirts or caps at an off-price store. Provide a variety of permanent markers and let the young teens write their blessings on their t-shirt or cap.

◎ Adapt the theme of the banner to fit other themes that you might be doing in a retreat or meeting. For example, the banner might list "Things that make me a good friend" for a session on friendship, "Things that make me a good Christian" for a class on discipleship, or "Reasons God loves me" for a retreat on building a relationship with God.

◎ Provide magazines and other craft materials and let the young teens find pictures and words to accompany each blessing and decorate their banner more fully.

◎ If you are doing this activity as part of an extended session and are providing a folder or booklet, suggest that the young people do their banner on the cover. This will help them all identify their folder or booklet easily and quickly.

NOTES

Use the space below to jot notes and reminders for the next time you use this strategy.

Suits Me!

OVERVIEW | Playing cards provide the means by which the young people engage in low-level self-disclosure, using predetermined conversation-starters. This activity works well for small-group formation and also as a periodic attention-getting activity during a retreat or a long session.

Suggested Time

A minimum of 5 minutes, depending on the size of the group and the number of rounds

Group Size

This strategy works with any size group, but if you have more than six partici-pants, you may want to forms smaller groups and provide each group with a deck of cards.

Materials Needed

- ☼ playing cards
- ☼ resource 5, "Conversation-Starters," on page 98
- ☼ newsprint and markers
- ☼ masking tape

PROCEDURE

Preparation. Choose four topics from resource 5 and assign each to one of the card suits. Or come up with your own conversation-starters that are directly related to the topic of your gathering. Be sure that you word each starter so that the same person can respond to it in a variety of ways, should someone be dealt the same suit more than once.

Draw the four suit symbols—heart, diamond, club, and spade—down the left side of a sheet of newsprint. Next to each symbol write the conversation-starter topic. Post the newsprint.

Shuffle the deck of cards, leaving in the jokers. Deal a card to one person at a time. The person must answer the corresponding conversation-starter before you deal a card to the next person. If you deal a joker to someone, the recipient may choose the topic. Go through as many rounds as you have time for.

ALTERNATIVE APPROACHES

◎ End the activity by letting everyone choose their own conversation-starter topic.
◎ Start with the grouper "It's in the Cards" on pages 22–24 of this manual. Begin the conversation in small groups by having everyone address the conversation-starter corresponding to the card they were dealt.

NOTES

Use the space below to jot notes and reminders for the next time you use this strategy.

I Am More Like . . .

This forced-choice activity helps the young people articulate and share some of their personal characteristics and develop an appreciation for differences among people.

Suggested Time

At least 5 minutes, depending on the size of the group and the number of pairs you present for consideration.

Group Size

This strategy works with any size group.

PROCEDURE

1. Gather the young people in the center of the room. Tell them that you will start with the phrase, "Are you more like," and give them two options, designating one side of the room for each option. They are to move to the side of the room that corresponds to the answer that most fits them. No one is allowed to stay in the middle. Tell them not to discuss their choice with anyone until after they move. Make it clear that you are asking about what they *are most like,* not what they *like.* You may need to give an example, especially to younger teens who are more likely to revert to personal preferences.

2. Read as many of the following pairs as you like, pointing to one side of the room for each option. After reading each pair, pause while everyone makes their choice, then ask a few people from each side to state the reasons for their choice.

Are you more like . . .
- a lightbulb . . . or a candle?
- a spark plug . . . or a battery?
- a library . . . or an amusement park?
- a table . . . or a chair?
- an automobile . . . or an airplane?
- a picture . . . or a puzzle?
- a hotel . . . or a hospital?
- the beach . . . or the mountains?
- a golf ball . . . or a Nerf ball?
- a sprinter . . . or a distance runner?
- a quarterback . . . or a left tackle?
- a bridge . . . or a tower?
- a magnifying glass . . . or a telescope?
- a paper clip . . . or a stapler?
- an oak tree . . . or an evergreen?
- a book . . . or a made-for-TV movie?
- a rowboat . . . or an ocean liner?
- a dictionary . . . or an encyclopedia?
- a fireplace . . . or a furnace?
- a telephone . . . or a television?

3. Close the exercise by commenting on the uniqueness of people's reasons, the fascinating workings of the human mind, and the wonder of God, who created it all.

ALTERNATIVE APPROACH

◎ At another point in the gathering, present the same pairs, but ask the participants to decide which one God is more like. Invite them to share their reasons for their choices.

NOTES

Use the space below to jot notes and reminders for the next time you use this strategy.

Pass the Basket

OVERVIEW This strategy gives the young teens an opportunity to share information about themselves at any level of self-disclosure—from the least threatening to the more risky. As the leader your task is to determine how deep to go. This is a good activity to begin a class or to build small-group trust on a retreat.

Suggested Time

The time it takes to do this strategy depends on the size of the group and the number of rounds of questions.

Group Size

This activity works with any size group.

Materials Needed

* ☼ a copy of resource 6, "Getting to Know You," with each page a different color
* ☼ a scissors
* ☼ baskets, bags, bowls, or other containers, one for each small group

PROCEDURE

Preparation. Decide which questions from resource 6 you will use. Note that each page of the handout contains questions that require a different level of self-disclosure, with level 1 being the least threatening. Cut apart the questions that you plan to use, fold them, and place several in a basket or other container for each group.

Gather the participants into groups of no more than eight people each. Place a container of questions in the middle of each group. Ask for a volunteer from each group to choose the first question, or designate someone to do so. If you are using more than one level of questions, tell the participants which color of paper to choose in the first round, that is, the color with the lowest level of personal disclosure.

Allow the young people to continue drawing questions as many times as your schedule allows. If you have used more than one level, progress to the color of slips that require more self-disclosure as you see fit. Be sure to answer a question yourself when it is your turn.

ALTERNATIVE APPROACHES

◎ Add a seasonal theme to the activity. Depending on the time of the year, you might enclose the questions in plastic Easter eggs or in jewelry gift boxes decorated for Christmas, tape them onto hearts for Valentine's Day, or wrap them around pencils for the beginning of the school year. Use your imagination and the resources at hand.
◎ You can find more questions like those on resource 6 in a variety of books, including *The Kids' Book of Questions,* by Gregory Stock (New York: Workman Publishing, 1988) and *What If . . . ?* by Les Christie (El Cajon, CA: Youth Specialties, 1996).

NOTES

Use the space below to jot notes and reminders for the next time you use this strategy.

Getting to Know You

Each page of this resource contains questions that require a different level of self-disclosure, with level 1 being the least threatening. Photocopy each level onto a different color of paper. Choose the questions that seem most appropriate for your group, cut them apart, fold them, and place several in a basket or other container for each group.

Level 1

What is your favorite season of the year?	Where is one of your favorite places to go with your friends?
What is your favorite sport to watch?	What is your favorite breakfast cereal?
What is your favorite sport to play?	What is your idea of a great weekend?
What is your favorite dessert?	Name one memorable teacher. What made her or him memorable?
What is one food you can't stand?	What is your favorite time of day? Why?
What is the best movie you have ever seen?	What is the best gift you have ever received?
What is the best vacation you have ever been on?	What is the most far-off place you have ever visited?
What is your favorite flavor of ice cream?	What do you like to do in your free time?
What career or profession would you least like to work in?	What is your favorite song?
What career or profession would you most like to work in?	What was the first movie you remember seeing?
What was your favorite toy as a child? Why?	What is one regular chore that you don't mind doing?
If you could grade your school, what grade would you give it?	What would your ultimate birthday party look like?

Level 2

If you could spend a day with a famous person (now living), whom would you choose? Why?	What is something you are proud of having done?
What three words would you use to describe God?	If you could trade lives with someone, who would you pick? Why?
If you were pope, what is the first thing you would change about the church if you could?	If you could have any talent, what would it be?
If you were president, what is one thing you would change about the country if you could?	If Jesus lived on earth today, what would most distress him?
Who has taught you the most about God?	What three words would your best friend use to describe you?
If you had the power to see into the future, what is one thing you would like to know?	What is one thing that really makes you angry?
If you had the power to solve one world problem, which one would you choose? Why?	What is one thing that makes you happy?
What do you think you will be doing in twenty years?	If you had twenty-five thousand dollars to give away, what would you do with it?
What question would you ask God if God were sitting next to you?	What is one fear you had as a child?
How would you describe heaven?	What are three qualities you want your friends to have?
If you were to be granted one magical power, what would you pick? Why?	What are three qualities you admire in your mom?
If you could be famous, what would you want to be known for?	What animal do you think you are most like? Why?
When was the last time you were generous to a stranger, just because you wanted to be nice?	Who is your favorite relative other than your parents? Why?
What is something that you love doing now, but probably will not enjoy in ten years?	What are three qualities you admire in your dad?
What is something that you love doing now, and probably will still enjoy in ten years?	What are two secrets for a long-lasting friendship?

Level 2 (continued)

What is the luckiest thing that ever happened to you?	What is the best thing you have done for someone younger than yourself?
What do you think life will be like in one hundred years?	What is the nicest thing you have ever done for a neighbor?
What cartoon character are you most like?	What day in your life would you like to live over again?
If you could not watch television for a year, what would you do with all the extra time?	What three things need to happen for you to have a really great day?
What is the best thing about being your age? the worst thing?	Who is the kindest person you ever met?
What is one privilege you do not have but wish you did?	When is the first time you remember winning at something? How did you feel?
What is the best surprise you ever got?	If you were invisible for one day, what would you do?
What is one responsibility you have that you do not like?	What do you think is the perfect age? Why?
What are two things that cause you stress?	What is your idea of a successful person?
What are two things for which you are thankful?	What is one thing you really miss about being a child?
If you could be the most attractive, the most athletic, the most popular, or the smartest person in your class, which would you choose? Why?	How does your best friend remind you of Jesus?
What is one thing you would like your mom or dad to say to you?	What is the best compliment you can receive?
If you could take a class and learn how to do anything, what class would you take? Why?	If your family were a comic strip, what strip would it be?
What is one funny family memory about you?	What is your favorite way to relax and get rid of stress?
What is one toy you always wanted as a child but never got?	What event in history would you like to observe firsthand? Why?

Level 3

What really frustrates you?	If you could begin one new tradition in your family, what would it be?
What is one thing that you really like about yourself?	If you could be your parents for a day, what would you do differently with you?
When do you feel lonely?	What would your life be like if you woke up tomorrow as a person of the other gender?
Where do you feel closest to God?	If you could relive one day of your life, which would it be? Why?
What is something that you fear?	If you could take back something you said to someone recently, what would it be?
What is something about your family that concerns you?	What would the world be missing if you hadn't been born?
When in the last month did you feel closest to your dad or mom?	How do you define the word *success?*
How do you feel about living forever?	How do you define the word *failure?*
What is one time when you have been aware of God's presence?	If you could surprise a loved one with a gift, what would it be? Why?
What is one question you have about being a Christian?	Who is a role model for you?
When and how do you pray best?	If you could change one decision you have made in your life, what would it be? Why?
What is one favorite memory of the time spent with your family as a child?	What is the bravest thing you ever did?
How long do you want to live? Why?	What question would you be afraid to ask someone because of the answer you might get?
Describe the last time you had a tough decision to make. What did you do?	What is the most important thing you have learned about life in the past year?
Who are three heroes in your life?	Which road sign is a symbol of your life?

Dominoes Admissions

This is another strategy that encourages the young people to share information about themselves. It uses the number of dots on dominoes to determine the admissions people are to make to the group.

Suggested Time

Depends on the number of people in the group and the number of rounds

Group Size

This activity works with any size group. However, if you have more than eight participants, divide them into smaller groups and give each small group a set of dominoes.

Materials Needed

- ☼ dominoes
- ☼ resource 7, "Admit One . . ."
- ☼ newsprint and markers
- ☼ masking tape

PROCEDURE

Preparation. Choose as many statements from resource 7 as the highest total number of dots on a domino in your set of dominoes (usually twelve or eighteen). The topics vary in the level of self-disclosure required; choose those that are appropriate to the level of familiarity and comfort in your group. Copy your chosen statements onto a sheet of newsprint, numbering each one.

Gather the young people in small groups of eight or fewer people. Place enough dominoes facedown in the middle of each group so that each person can choose a new one during each round. That is, if you are planning on three rounds and you have seven members in a group, give that group twenty-one dominoes.

Designate one person from each group to choose a domino and add up the number of dots on the face of it. That person should "admit one" item that corresponds to that number on the newsprint list. Go around the group as often as time and interest allow.

ALTERNATIVE APPROACH

 Eliminate the dominoes and make a copy of resource 7 for every participant. Starting with yourself, admit one thing on the list, then ask someone else in the group to admit the same thing. After doing so, that person chooses another item, admits it, and asks someone else in the group to admit the same thing. The process continues, with the turn passing to someone new each time, until everyone has had a chance to admit something.

NOTES

Use the space below to jot notes and reminders for the next time you use this strategy.

Admit One . . .

☀ person who makes you laugh

☀ thing you keep under your bed

☀ law you would establish if you could

☀ wonderful thing someone has told you

☀ thing that made you angry in the last week

☀ good risk you have taken

☀ place you would live if you could

☀ boring activity you dread doing

☀ Bible character you would be afraid to meet

☀ public figure you think is strange

☀ thing you need prayer for

☀ thing you like about your mom

☀ class you secretly like

☀ thing you wish you had never said

☀ time you felt lonely

☀ thing you would like your parents to say to you

☀ reason you like your best friend

☀ thing that makes you feel afraid

☀ sound that drives you crazy

☀ thing you do that makes you angry with yourself

☀ time you were thankful to God

☀ time God answered your prayers

☀ thing that makes you sad

☀ concern you have for the world

☀ thing you want to pass down to your children

Shed a Little Light

This strategy gets the young teens sharing some of their stories with a variety of people. It is a good activity for extended sessions, retreats, or any time you want the young people to get to know one another in a different way. It can also be adapted to a variety of situations, depending on the needs of the group.

Suggested Time

10 to 20 minutes

Group Size

This strategy works with any size group.

Materials Needed

- construction paper in three to five different colors
- a scissors

PROCEDURE

Preparation. Make a lightbulb shape out of construction paper for each young person. Use three to five different colors of paper, depending on the size of your group. The smaller the group, the fewer colors you will need. Be sure to have approximately equal numbers of lightbulbs in each color.

1. Distribute the colored lightbulbs that you prepared. Explain that when we tell other people stories about things that happen in our life, we shed a little light on who we are and get to know everyone else a little better.

2. Direct the young people to form groups, with one of each color of lightbulb in each group. If some people are left out, add them to existing groups. When everyone has found a group, ask them to share with one another their name and something about themselves. Focus their sharing by having them tell about one of the following topics:

a time when you used a personal skill to help someone out

what you remember most about the first day of school this year

a fun time your family had together this past summer

at the age of five, what you wanted to be when you grew up

a time when you really felt successful at something

You may want to designate someone to begin by using the strategy "Fifty Ways to Choose a Leader" on pages 48–50.

The level of disclosure in this activity can be as nonthreatening or as risky as the group is ready for. Consult the list of topics in resource 6, "Getting to Know You," on pages 110–113, for other possibilities. Assure the participants that they will not have to speak longer than 30 seconds.

3. After a minute, tell everyone to mix into new small groups, this time with those who have the same color lightbulb. Go through the process as many times as you can. Another possible grouping is to include two of each color of light-bulb. Or tell everyone to exchange lightbulbs and start the activity again.

ALTERNATIVE APPROACHES

◎ Use the lightbulbs as name tags. Distribute them when the young people arrive, along with pins or double-stick tape.

◎ Do an emotional check-in with the group while also facilitating the interaction. Give everyone a pen or a pencil and direct them each to write in large numbers on their bulb a wattage that reflects the kind of week they had. Identify on newsprint the typical wattages of household bulbs: 15, 25, 40, 60, 75, 100; 125, and 150. A 15-watt bulb would mean that that person's week was awful. A 150-watt bulb would indicate that that person had a fabulous week.

◎ Open or close your class or session with a prayer that includes a reflection on Matt. 5:14–16 (Let your light shine).

NOTES

Use the space below to jot notes and reminders for the next time you use this strategy.

(This strategy is adapted from *Growing Close,* edited by Stephen Parolini, pp. 53–54.)

Who's Your Neighbor?

The young people are asked to answer questions about their neighbor as they think their neighbor would answer them. The neighbor gets a chance to correct and clarify any misconceptions or misinformation. This is a good activity for young teens who know one another somewhat but want to become closer.

Suggested Time

10 to 20 minutes

Group Size

This strategy works best with groups no larger than twenty people. If you have more participants than that, you may want to form smaller groups.

PROCEDURE

1. Gather the participants in a circle. Try to arrange the circle so that good friends are not sitting next to one another. Tell everyone that you will ask each of them a question. They are to respond as they think the neighbor on their right would respond. If they are not sure, they should take a guess. Caution them to be kind to each other, not to put each other down, and so forth.

2. Read one of the following questions to the person on your right and ask him or her to respond. Give the neighbor a chance to clarify and correct the answer. Then instruct the neighbor to answer the question, and so forth. Get around the circle at least once, or as far as time allows.

- What sport does your neighbor most enjoy participating in?
- What is your neighbor's favorite television show?
- If your neighbor had a free afternoon, what would he [or she] do?
- What musical instrument or instruments can your neighbor play?
- Is your neighbor a morning person or an evening person?
- What does your neighbor like about herself [or himself]?
- What is your neighbor most proud of?
- If your neighbor had a million dollars, what would he [or she] do with it?
- What really bores your neighbor?
- What is your neighbor looking forward to doing in the next six months?
- What is your neighbor really good at?
- If your neighbor could have any job, what would it be?
- What does one of your neighbor's parents do for a living?
- What television star would your neighbor like to be?
- What really frustrates your neighbor?
- What would your neighbor like to do someday that he [or she] has not yet done?
- If your neighbor could work at any job, what would it be?
- What talent does your neighbor wish he [or she] had?

ALTERNATIVE APPROACHES

- Before doing this exercise, do one of the other get-to-know-you activities in part C so that people can find out some things about one another.
- Create your own questions based on the questions in resource 6, "Getting to Know You," on pages 110–113.

NOTES

Use the space below to jot notes and reminders for the next time you use this strategy.

(This strategy is adapted from *Building Community in Youth Groups,* by Denny Rydberg, pp. 75–76.)

Sharing Board Game

OVERVIEW

This strategy uses the format of a board game to facilitate sharing and discussion among young people. This is a good format for retreats, extended sessions, or any gathering where helping the participants get to know one another is the primary goal.

Suggested Time

At least 20 minutes

Group Size

This activity works with any size group, divided into small groups of eight or fewer.

Materials Needed

- ☼ resource 5, "Conversation-Starters," on page 98, or resource 6, "Getting to Know You," on pages 110–113
- ☼ 3-by-5-inch index cards, about twenty for each small group
- ☼ dice, one for each small group
- ☼ buttons, beads, beans, small toys, or something else to use as game pieces, a distinctive one for each person

PROCEDURE

Preparation. Make a set of game cards for each small group as follows: Choose about twenty conversation-starters or questions from resource 5 or 6. Select them based on the comfort level of your group and what you want to accomplish. Write each starter or question on a separate index card. Make a few cards that are typical of board games, such as "Jump ahead two spaces" or "Go in the opposite direction." Use your imagination. Intersperse these cards with the rest.

1. Form small groups of no more than eight people each. Give each small group a set of game cards, a die, and one place marker for each person. Tell the groups each to arrange their index cards in the form of a game board, with one card adjacent to another.

2. When each small group has made its own game board, designate someone in the group (e.g., the person whose birthday is closest to today's date) to begin by throwing the die and moving that many spaces. That person has 30 seconds or less to respond to the starter or question she or he landed on. After the first person is done, the second person rolls the die, and so forth.

This game has no end, except as dictated by time and interest. Keep a close eye on both.

ALTERNATIVE APPROACHES

◎ Write the questions on large pieces of paper or poster board, arrange them on the floor, and let the young people be their own game piece, moving the number of spaces on the die.

◎ Use this format for reviewing class material, changing the questions to reflect whatever topics the young teens have learned about in your program.

NOTES

Use the space below to jot notes and reminders for the next time you use this strategy.

(This strategy is adapted from *FaithWays,* by Mary Lee Becker, pp. 29 and 33.)

Four Corners

This forced-choice exercise not only gets the young people moving around but also puts them in a situation with people who think like they do. For a young teen who may feel like he or she does not belong, membership in a group like this—no matter how temporary—can be very affirming.

Suggested Time

At least 10 minutes, but the exercise can go on as long as you want it to

Group Size

This strategy works with any size group.

Materials Needed

- four 8½-by-11-inch, or larger, sheets of paper
- a marker
- masking tape

PROCEDURE

Preparation. Write in large, bold print the letters *A, B, C,* and *D* each on a separate sheet of paper. Post the papers, one in each of four corners of the room, at a height that makes them visible to all.

1. Gather the young people in the middle of the room. Tell them that you will read a sentence-starter and four possible answers. They are to think about how they would finish the sentence and move to the corner with the sign that corresponds to the letter of the answer that most closely represents their choice.

2. Read the first sentence-starter and its four choices. Be clear about which answer corresponds to each corner. You may have to read the choices more than once.

Some sample statements follow. They are grouped by the level of self-disclosure they require, with level 1 being the least threatening. You may want to create your own statements to more closely meet the needs of your group.

Level 1

When I am able to drive, I would like to own a . . .
- **a.** pickup truck
- **b.** Volkswagen bug
- **c.** BMW
- **d.** sports car

My idea of a good book is a . . .
- **a.** comic book
- **b.** science fiction book
- **c.** romance
- **d.** biography of a famous person

At home the thing that annoys me most is . . .
- **a.** having to keep my room clean
- **b.** having someone look around my room
- **c.** having to do chores
- **d.** having restrictions on television, phone, or computer time

To me, an ideal vacation would be . . .
- **a.** visiting Hawaii
- **b.** visiting friends or relatives out of town
- **c.** skiing
- **d.** camping

On television I most like to watch . . .
- **a.** sports
- **b.** music videos
- **c.** comedy
- **d.** drama

Level 2

When I have a disagreement with someone, I usually . . .

    a. want to discuss it with the person

    b. keep it inside

    c. talk to other friends about it

    d. blow up and have an argument

If I have to be stereotyped, I would rather be thought of as . . .

    a. warm, friendly, and caring

    b. cool, calm, and collected

    c. vibrant, fun, and in search of a good time

    d. serious, thoughtful, and wise

What the world needs most right now is . . .

    a. love and compassion

    b. food for all

    c. an end to all wars

    d. justice

When I think about my life fifteen years from now, I see myself . . .

    a. married, with children

    b. in school, pursuing a professional or graduate degree

    c. on my own, working at a job

    d. living with my parents

When I'm under a lot of stress, I look for someone to help me out of it . . .

    a. always

    b. frequently

    c. once in a while

    d. never

Level 3

The question of whether God really exists is on my mind . . .

    a. always

    b. frequently

    c. once in a while

    d. never

If I found out I had only six months to live, I would . . .

    a. not tell anyone and would go about my life as usual

    b. leave school and spend all my time with my family and friends

    c. do something crazy that I've always wanted to do

    d. avoid as much human contact as possible

The thing I worry most about is . . .

    a. grades

    b. my parents' relationship

    c. my friends and what they expect of me

    d. the future

Today I'm feeling . . .
    a. bored
    b. happy
    c. nervous
    d. kind of down
My best quality is my . . .
    a. intelligence
    b. sense of humor
    c. drive and sense of purpose
    d. compassion for others

3. Let the participants discuss their choice with others who made the same choice, giving examples, sharing stories, and so forth.

ALTERNATIVE APPROACH

◎ You may want to add a fifth possible answer—"none of the above." The people who choose that answer would stay in the middle of the room.

NOTES

Use the space below to jot notes and reminders for the next time you use this strategy.

Four Sharing Formats

OVERVIEW The four strategies in this section facilitate sharing between partners or in small groups. They are quite similar in process, but some are more suitable depending on the space you have available.

Suggested Time

The time depends on the size of the group and the number of questions you want the young people to discuss.

Group Size

These strategies work best with groups larger than ten people.

Materials Needed

All four strategies require resource 6, "Getting to Know You," on pages 110–113. Other supplies you will need are as follows:

For "Appointment Calendar"
- ☼ copies of handout 8, "Appointment Calendar," on page 131, one for each person
- ☼ pens or pencils

For "Sharing Cubes"
- ☼ foam, wood, or paper cubes, one for every six people
- ☼ a pen or a thin-line marker
- ☼ paper

a scissors
 glue or tape

SUGGESTED STRATEGIES

Parallel Pairs

Use one of the grouping activities in part A of this manual to form pairs. If you have an odd number of participants, include yourself or another adult in the mix.

Tell the pairs to form two parallel lines so that the partners are in different lines. Direct everyone to sit down facing their partner. Explain that you will lead them through a sharing exercise in which you ask a question and they respond to their partner for a certain amount of time. Designate which line of people will be the first speakers and tell them how long they have to answer the question. It is best to keep the time short to avoid awkward periods of silence. Assure them that you will announce when it is time for their partner to speak. Ask one of the questions from resource 6 and guide the process as just described.

After each side has had a chance to answer, instruct one side to move a certain number of people in a certain direction—for example, three people to the left. The people at one end of the line who do not get a partner as a result of the move should fill in the spaces at the other end of the line.

Continue as long as time and interest allow.

Circle Chums

Form pairs using one of the grouping activities in part A of this manual. If you have an odd number of participants, include yourself or another adult in the mix. Have the pairs form two concentric circles with the partners in different circles, facing each other. Follow the process outlined in the previous activity, "Parallel Pairs," except that when it comes time to shift, direct either the inner circle or the outer circle to move a certain number of people in a certain direction.

Appointment Calendar

This is an excellent get-to-know-you activity for a retreat or an extended session. It works best in a group where the young people know one another or are not afraid to mix and mingle on their own.

Give everyone a copy of handout 8 and a pen or a pencil. Announce that they will be making appointments with various partners that they will meet with throughout the day.

Direct them to find a partner for each time slot and have that person sign her or his name. It is important that the partners sign each other's sheets for the same time slot. Otherwise they may schedule themselves to meet with someone else at that time. If you have some people who are not able to get a partner for a specific time slot, ask other adults to fill the gaps or meet with those people yourself.

After everyone has filled in their appointment calendar, call out a time slot by saying something like, "Find your 8 a.m. appointment." When everyone has found their 8 a.m. partner, read aloud a question from resource 6 and tell them to share their answer with their partner.

Return to the appointment calendar periodically throughout the session or the retreat, as time allows and energy dictates.

Sharing Cubes

You will need a cube for every six to eight people in your group. You can purchase foam or wood cubes at craft stores. Gift boxes that are made for mugs are also suitable for this activity.

Write questions from resource 6, one each on pieces of paper the size of a side of your cubes. Attach one question to each side of the cubes. Form the young people into groups of six to eight people and have them gather into circles. Give each group a cube and tell the group members to take turns rolling the cube and answering the question that comes up. Rotate the cubes among the groups as time allows.

ALTERNATIVE APPROACHES

◎ Before using any of these sharing strategies, do a game or two to increase the comfort level of the group. Games that get partners to work together would be especially helpful. Check the bibliography in the introduction for books about games and community-building ideas.

◎ *For "Sharing Cubes."* Instead of cubes use regular dice, and for each group write on newsprint six questions, numbered 1 to 6 to correspond to the number of dots on the different sides of the dice. To add a little more variety, for each group use two dice and provide twelve questions.

NOTES

Use the space below to jot notes and reminders for the next time you use this strategy.

Appointment Calendar

Find a partner for each of the time slots listed on the clock below. When you find someone with the same empty time slot as you have, sign each other's papers in that spot. Your leader will tell you when it is time to meet with that person.

It is important that you and your partner sign each other's appointment sheet for the same time slot. Otherwise you will be looking for different people when that appointment time is announced.

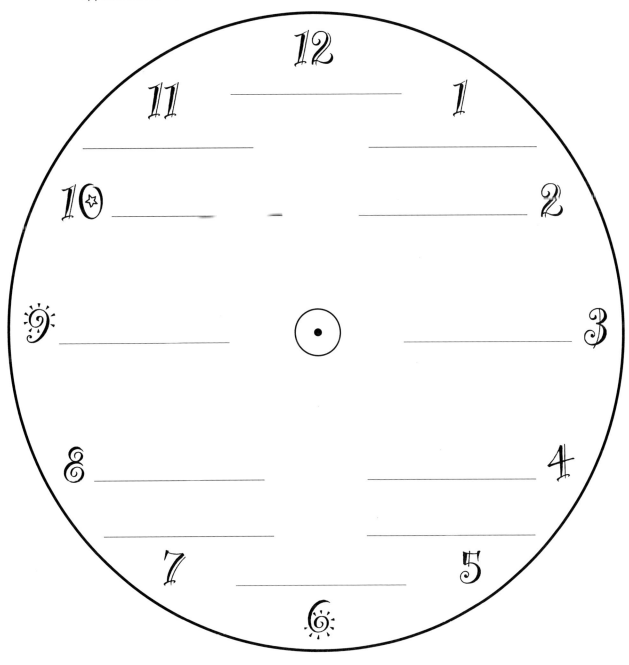

Part D
Building Teams

A strong team is critical to the success of a group or a project. Young teens tend to be wary of giving too much information or putting forth too much effort, unless they are reasonably sure that they are contributing to the endeavor in a meaningful way. They want to know that they are valuable, that they have something important to contribute, and that their efforts are appreciated.

The activities in this section can help build a sense of unity among young teens. Some of the activities involve problem solving, some are competitive, some are quiet and reflective, and some are noisy, but they are all fun ways to create a sense of community and belonging.

Blind Lineup

OVERVIEW

This problem-solving strategy forces the young people to use different forms of communication to accomplish a task. It is an ideal activity for the outdoors, but works indoors as well.

Suggested Time

About 15 minutes

Group Size

This strategy works best with groups of twenty people or fewer. If you have more than twenty participants, form smaller groups of ten to fifteen people and provide each group with a log, a bench, or a facsimile of a log or a bench.

Materials Needed

- ☼ a log, a bench, or materials to create a facsimile of a log or a bench
- ☼ blindfolds, one for each person

PROCEDURE

Preparation. This activity can be conducted outside or inside. You will need a long log or a long bench without a back. If a suitable log or bench is not available, you can create a facsimile of one. For example, you might put two parallel strips of masking tape on the floor, about 15 inches apart, using about 18 inches of tape for each person in the group. Outside, you might draw the lines with sidewalk chalk.

1. Direct everyone to line up standing on a log, on a bench, or perhaps between two parallel lines of tape or chalk. Give everyone a blindfold and tell them to put it on. Explain that their task is to arrange themselves in a certain order on the log, on the bench, or within the parallel lines. The only stipulation is that they must remain blindfolded for the entire activity. If they fall off the log or the bench or step outside the lines, they must go to the end of the line in the opposite direction from where they were headed.

If you are using lines on the floor or ground, appoint other adults to watch for people who step out of the lines.

2. When everyone has their blindfold in place, tell them to line up in alphabetical order (decide whether it should be according to first or last names). Emphasize that they must stay on the log, on the bench, or between the lines. If they cannot, they must move to the end of the line in the opposite direction from where they were heading.

If you have time for a second round, tell the young teens to line up in order of birthdays or some other criteria that is objective. Do not use physical characteristics such as height or size of feet for this exercise because young teens may be self-conscious about such things.

3. Lead a discussion of the following questions:

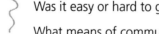

Was it easy or hard to get started with this exercise? Why?

What means of communication did your group use?

Who emerged as the leaders in your group?

What did this exercise teach you about communication?

4. Close the exercise by commenting on the young people's communication, teamwork, and ability to get the task accomplished in less-than-ideal circumstances.

ALTERNATIVE APPROACHES

◉ For an added challenge, tell the young people to line up without talking.

◉ For blindfolds you can use dark-colored construction paper. For each person cut out a rectangle of about 9-by-4 inches. Cut a V for the nose, and fasten the blindfold with a rubber band around the head.

SCRIPTURAL CONNECTIONS

◉ Rom. 8:28–29 (All things work together for good.)

◉ Matt. 18:19–20 (Where people gather, God is in their midst.)

◉ Acts 2:46–47 (The disciples worked together and prayed together every day.)

◉ Rom. 12:1–8 (We have different gifts to use for good.)

NOTES

Use the space below to jot notes and reminders for the next time you use this strategy.

(This strategy is adapted from *Building Community in Youth Groups,* by Denny Rydberg, pp. 34–35.)

Human Sculptures

This strategy challenges the young adolescents to work as a team to mimic common items and machines, using only their bodies. This is a good exercise to bring down group barriers because everyone on the team has to be involved in some way.

Suggested Time

About 20 minutes

Group Size

This strategy works with any size group, but the sculptures must be created in teams no larger than six people.

Materials Needed

- index cards or small pieces of paper, at least one for each team
- a pen or a pencil

PROCEDURE

Preparation. Write one of each of the following items on an index card or a piece of paper. You will need at least one item for every six people in your group. If you have more than sixty participants, think of additional similar items, and create cards or papers for them as well.

- dump truck
- washing machine
- telephone booth
- sewing machine
- hot air balloon
- snowplow
- elevator
- garbage disposal
- school bus
- grandfather clock

1. Divide the participants into small groups of no more than six people. Tell them that their group will be given a card or a piece of paper with an item written on it. They are not to show that item to any other group. Their task is to prepare and present a human sculpture pantomime of their item. The group can use only group members' bodies and sound effects to form the sculpture. Props are not allowed. Everyone in the group must be involved in some way in the sculpture.

2. Give each group one of the cards or pieces or paper. Announce that everyone has 10 minutes to prepare their sculpture. If possible send each group to a different room to prepare.

3. After 10 minutes call the groups back together. Have them take turns presenting their human sculpture to the other groups. After each performance encourage the rest of the young teens to guess what item was being depicted.
    If time allows let each group prepare and present a second sculpture.

4. Lead a discussion on the following questions:

Who in the group came up with at least one creative idea for the sculpture?

How did it feel to be planning something like this together?

How did it feel when you presented the sculpture together?

How is doing this human sculpture like being part of a family, a church, an athletic team, or a performing group?

5. Close the activity by commenting on the young people's creativity, imagination, and problem-solving abilities.

ALTERNATIVE APPROACH

◉ Challenge the groups to come up with their own idea for a pantomime. Set certain criteria, such as it must be a machine, it must be used in a house or a school, it must be something one uses on vacation, and so forth. You may want to allow a little more time for preparation because they have to come up with an item before they figure out how to pantomime it.

SCRIPTURAL CONNECTIONS

◉ Rom. 12:1–8 (We each have different gifts.)
◉ 1 Cor. 12:12–13 (We are members of one body.)
◉ Gal. 3:28 (We are equal in our Baptism.)

NOTES

Use the space below to jot notes and reminders for the next time you use this strategy.

(This strategy is adapted from *FaithWays,* by Mary Lee Becker, p. 47.)

Over the Wall

OVERVIEW

This strategy requires the young teens to do some brainstorming and problem solving together. They must figure out how to get every member of the group over a wall using nothing but themselves. It is particularly good as an outdoor activity, but can work indoors also.

Suggested Time

About 20 minutes

Group Size

This strategy can be done with any size group, divided into small groups of five to eight people.

Special Considerations

Young people who are extremely self-conscious about their body will not do well with this exercise. If some of the young teens in your group seem to be self-conscious about their height or weight or other physical characteristics, you may want to try another exercise.

Be sure to have enough adults helping out so that each group has an adult spotter to keep an eye out for safety.

Materials Needed

- ☼ rope or string
- ☼ items or structures that you can secure rope or string to at a height of about 4 feet

PROCEDURE

Preparation. This strategy involves creating an imaginary wall for each small group. To make a wall, run a string about 4 feet off the ground between two trees, two poles, or other stationary objects. The space under the string does not have to be filled.

1. Divide the participants into groups of five to eight people. Tell everyone to stand with their group on one side of their wall. When everyone is in place, explain the following directions:

The group's task is to get everyone over the rope wall safely. No one can go under the rope or around the sides. Avoid touching the rope at all.

No one can get herself or himself over the wall. That is, no hurdling or high jumping is allowed.

If someone who made it over the wall wants to go back and help someone else get over the wall, he or she must be helped back over the wall to the starting side.

Emphasize the need to pay attention to safety issues. Be sure to have an adult with each group to act as a spotter. Also point out that this activity is not a competition. It is a problem-solving activity. So nothing is to be gained by the group that finishes first.

2. When the young people are ready, start the process. Pay attention to their levels of communication and creativity when it comes to problem solving.

3. When all the groups have accomplished the task, bring them together in a circle and discuss the following questions:

What were some of the solutions?

How did you feel while you were being helped over the wall?

How did your team work together? Was everyone involved? Did some people lead more than others?

How is this activity like being part of a family? a team? a church?

4. Close with an affirmation of the teams' good work, creativity, attention to safety, and so forth.

ALTERNATIVE APPROACHES

◎ To make this exercise even more difficult, have the groups get over the wall in silence. Or allow 5 minutes of talking at the beginning so that they can plan their strategy, and then require silence.

◎ Follow this exercise with a prayer service on the themes of community, leadership, vulnerability, and service.

SCRIPTURAL CONNECTIONS

◎ Luke 8:16–18 (Do not hide your gifts.)
◎ Col. 3:12–17 (Support one another in the name of God.)
◎ Eph. 4:17—5:2 (Rules for Christian living)

NOTES

Use the space below to jot notes and reminders for the next time you use this strategy.

(This strategy is adapted from *Building Community in Youth Groups,* by Denny Rydberg, pp. 37–38.)

Spaghetti Towers

OVERVIEW This strategy challenges the young teens to work as a team to build a structure using only spaghetti and marshmallows. It is a good activity to use on retreat and when discussing themes of church and community.

Suggested Time

About 20 minutes

Group Size

This strategy works with any size group, divided into small groups of no more than eight people.

Materials Needed

- ☼ old newspapers, one full sheet for each small group
- ☼ 1-pound boxes of spaghetti, one for each small group
- ☼ bags of large marshmallows, one for each small group

PROCEDURE

1. If your group is larger than eight, divide the participants into small groups of no more than eight. Give each small group a sheet of newspaper, a box of spaghetti, and a bag of marshmallows. Tell everyone to put the paper on the floor or table in the middle of their group. Then explain the activity as follows:

> Your task as a group is to create the highest, most beautiful freestanding structure that you can using only spaghetti, marshmallows, and ingenuity.

> You may not move around or look at what other groups are doing. You must stay with your structure until the judging.

2. Once the participants know the rules, give them a signal to begin. Observe how they work together, who is coming up with ideas, who is standing back, and so forth. Allow about 10 minutes for the groups to work.

3. When time is up, ask the young teens to walk around and look at one another's structures. Choose one tower as the winner based on the criteria outlined above: it must be the highest, it must be freestanding, and it must be attractive—relatively speaking!

4. Follow the activity with discussion questions such as these:

> How did you like working with the materials?

> Who in your group had the most ideas? Who was the leader? Who was the doer? Did anyone just sit back and not participate?

> How is this activity like being part of a church or another faith community?

> How does this activity relate to God and us?

5. Close the activity by thanking the young people for their cooperation, enthusiasm, and ideas and by challenging them to pitch in and help the next time a task needs to be accomplished.

Ask the young people to carefully fold up their structures into the newspapers and put them in the trash.

ALTERNATIVE APPROACHES

◎ Close by carefully sliding all the structures to the middle of the room. Ask some young people to attach all the structures using additional spaghetti and marshmallows. While they are doing that, comment on how each structure represents part of the church in the world and that together all the structures make up the universal church. Do a prayer service on the theme of being church in the world.

◎ Invite the pastor, a parish council representative, or another official representative of the parish community to judge the structures and to stay for the prayer.

SCRIPTURAL CONNECTIONS

◎ Acts 2:43–47 (Being a Christian community)
◎ Luke 10:1–9 (Our mission is to bring Christ to the world.)
◎ Matt. 28:16–20 (Make disciples of all nations.)
◎ Acts 2:1–13 (The coming of the Holy Spirit)
◎ Matt. 25:14–30 (Use your talents wisely.)

NOTES

Use the space below to jot notes and reminders for the next time you use this strategy.

(This strategy is adapted from *Building Community in Youth Groups,* by Denny Rydberg, pp. 39–40.)

Jesus Jingles

OVERVIEW The young people turn famous commercial slogans into advertisements for God. This strategy draws on the participants' knowledge of media and their creativity with language.

Suggested Time

About 15 minutes

Group Size

This strategy can be done with any size group, divided into small groups of no more than eight.

Materials Needed

- ☼ newsprint, one sheet for each small group
- ☼ markers
- ☼ 8½-by-11-inch sheets of scrap paper, one for each person
- ☼ pens or pencils
- ☼ small prizes (optional)

PROCEDURE

1. If your group is larger than eight, form smaller groups. Give each small group a sheet of newsprint and some markers, and give each person a sheet of scrap paper and a pen or a pencil. Choose a leader for each group. You may want to look at "Fifty Ways to Choose a Leader" on pages 48–50 for ideas.

2. Ask the young people to name some popular commercial slogans or songs that they hear on television or the radio. After a few volunteers have offered suggestions, tell the young teens that their job is to brainstorm as many commercial slogans as they can. Then they must figure out how they can make the slogans be advertisements for Jesus. In some cases no change will be necessary—as, for example, with the Toyota slogan "Oh, what a feeling!" Other slogans will need just a slight change—for example, the answer to the question, "How do you spell relief?" might become, *"J-E-S-U-S."*

Explain that if the young people want to begin by brainstorming slogans individually, they can do so on the scrap paper. Eventually they must list on their team's newsprint as many Jesus jingles as they can. Also tell them that the team with the most jingles at the end of the allotted time is the winner.

3. Allow a minimum of 10 minutes for the groups to brainstorm slogans and rewrite them. Then ask a spokesperson for each group to present his or her group's results, or do so yourself.

You may want to award a small prize for the longest list, the most creative jingle, the most diverse products represented, and so forth.

4. Lead a discussion around these or similar questions:

Why do companies advertise?

What is your favorite commercial? your least favorite?

What is something that you have purchased because you saw it advertised in a magazine or on television? Was it all that the ad said it would be?

What can people do to get the word out about Jesus so that everyone wants to be a part of his message?

5. Close the activity by emphasizing the effect of advertising in our society and the need to look at commercials and ads critically. Also point out the need to let other people know about Jesus in every way possible, so that they can share in the gift of faith.

ALTERNATIVE APPROACHES

◎ Instead of telling the participants to change the slogans into advertisements for God, have them change the slogans into advertisements for your parish, school, or youth group.

◎ Direct each group to choose one commercial to plan and act out for the rest of the group.

◎ Follow this team-building exercise with a discussion of the effect of media on young people.

SCRIPTURAL CONNECTIONS

◎ John 20:16–18 (Mary Magdalene announces Jesus' Resurrection.)

◎ John 17:6–8 (Jesus gave us the word. Now it is ours to spread.)

◎ Matt: 10:5–8 (The work of a disciple is to spread the Good News.)

◎ Isa. 61:1–2 (We are anointed to bring good news to the world.)

◎ Ps. 89:1–5 (Proclaim God's faithfulness.)

NOTES

Use the space below to jot notes and reminders for the next time you use this strategy.

Yert Circle

OVERVIEW

In this team-building activity, the group creates a "yert circle," in which everyone must participate to their fullest, or everyone ends up on the floor. This is a good activity for a wide, open space. It addresses the topics of teamwork, holding one's own, and trust.

Suggested Time

About 10 minutes

Group Size

Six to sixty

PROCEDURE

1. Gather the young people in a circle, and designate each person an In or an Out, alternating around the circle. If the last person is an In, put yourself or another adult leader between him or her and the first In so that the pattern of alternating categories is unbroken.

2. Tell the young people that they are going to form what is known as a yert circle, in which the members of the circle hold one another up while moving. Ask the young teens to hold hands with the people on either side of them. Tell them to hold on tight, or else they may end up on the floor. Explain that when you say, "Go," the people who are Ins should lean into the circle while the people who are Outs should lean back. Note that everyone must lean from their ankles, not from their waist. They will hold up one another just by leaning in and out.

You may want to try a few dry runs, just until everyone gets the hang of it. After you are sure that they know what to do, start the game officially. Call out, "Switch," each time you want the group members to reverse the direction they are leaning. Get them moving in and out, first slowly, pausing about 10 seconds after each change so that they can get their bearings. Then start picking up the pace until the group is able to switch positions every 2 or 3 seconds.

3. End the activity with a discussion of the following questions:

What would have happened if one person had moved in when he or she was supposed to move out?

How did it feel to be dependent on another person?

How did it feel to have another person dependent on you?

Was it hard or easy to trust your neighbors in this activity? Why?

Is it hard or easy to trust God? Why?

ALTERNATIVE APPROACHES

◎ Instead of using the simple designations In and Out, use more creative combinations, like Hee and Haw, or Zig and Zag.
◎ Follow this activity with a prayer service on holding one another up and taking care of one another.

SCRIPTURAL CONNECTIONS

◎ 3 John, verses 5–8 (Support those who do God's work with you.)
◎ Col. 3:12–17 (Support and encourage one another.)
◎ Rom. 8:28–29 (All things work together for good.)

NOTES

Use the space below to jot notes and reminders for the next time you use this strategy.

(This activity is adapted from *Youth Group Trust Builders,* by Denny Rydberg, pp. 34–35.)

Group Juggling

The young people try to keep many objects traveling in the same pattern around their group at the same time. This strategy is a fun exercise in teamwork and highlights both the joys and frustrations of working together.

Suggested Time

10 to 15 minutes

Group Size

This strategy can be done with any size group, divided into smaller groups of five to eight people.

Materials Needed

- ☼ a few tossable objects (e.g., balls, rolled socks, oranges, cans of soup) for people who cannot find one among their belongings or elsewhere in the room

PROCEDURE

1. Announce that everyone must find a tossable object somewhere among their belongings or elsewhere in the room. Have a pile of extras available for those who cannot find anything. If the young teens are not already in small groups, form them into groups of five to eight. Tell the participants to gather in a circle with their group, with their object in front of them.

2. Choose one person from each group to start the juggling. Tell everyone in the group to give their object to that person. The leader tosses one object to another person in the group, who catches it and tosses it to another, and so forth. Every person in the group must catch and throw the object, until it gets back to the leader, establishing a juggling pattern that will be followed for all the objects. The only pattern that is not allowed is going around the circle from person to person.

Allow the groups to toss the first object around the pattern until they are comfortable with it. Then direct the leader to toss in a second object, keeping the same pattern. After a little while, a third object gets tossed in, and then a fourth, and so on, until the group is juggling all the objects at the same time.

3. After all the objects get back to the starter, lead a discussion using the following questions:

How did you feel when only one object was being tossed around?

How did you feel when all the objects were in the air?

What was the best thing about working as a team?

What was most frustrating about this activity?

What did this exercise have to do with being part of a family or a church?

4. Conclude with a prayer of thanksgiving for all the people who do their part to make things work well in families, in churches, and in communities.

ALTERNATIVE APPROACH

◎ Conclude the exercise by having every group toss an object again, in the same pattern. This time, however, before a person throws the object to someone, he or she must thank God for the person who just tossed the object to him or her.

SCRIPTURAL CONNECTIONS

◉ Phil. 1:3–6,9–11 (You have begun good work. You must continue.)
◉ 1 Cor. 12:12–31 (The body must work together.)
◉ Acts 2:43–47 (Living as a Christian community)

NOTES

Use the space below to jot notes and reminders for the next time you use this strategy.

(This strategy is adapted from *Do It!* by Thom Schultz and Joani Schultz, pp. 80–81.)

Look Very Closely

OVERVIEW This strategy tests the young teens' ability to observe another person and notice when something has changed. It is a good exercise to begin a session on communication or on teamwork.

Suggested Time

About 5 minutes

Group Size

This strategy works with any size group.

PROCEDURE

1. Have the young people divide into pairs. You may want to use one of the grouping exercises in part A.

Tell the participants to sit facing their partner and observe her or him for 1 minute. They are not to talk during this time, just to observe.

2. After a minute tell the partners to turn away from each other and sit back-to-back. Quietly and carefully, they should change one thing about themselves. For example, they might remove an earring, put their watch on the other arm, untie a shoe, and so forth. Allow about 30 seconds for them to make the change.

3. Direct the young teens to face their partner once again. This time they are to guess what is different about their partner. If they cannot guess after about 45 seconds, tell the partners to reveal the change.

If you have time, switch partners and do the exercise again.

4. Conclude by reminding the young teens of the importance of paying close attention to other people. It is only when we do so that we can pick up the subtle details.

SCRIPTURAL CONNECTIONS

- ◎ Psalm 139 (God knows everything about us.)
- ◎ 2 Cor. 5:1–5 (What is on the inside counts more than what is on the outside.)
- ◎ Mark 10:17–22 (Jesus calls us to change on the inside.)
- ◎ Psalm 19 (Be attentive to the glory of God's creation.)

NOTES

Use the space below to jot notes and reminders for the next time you use this strategy.

(This strategy is adapted from *FaithWays*, by Mary Lee Becker, pp. 5–6.)

Stand in the Square

OVERVIEW

This strategy tests the young teens' problem-solving abilities by asking them to find a way to get an entire group inside a 3-by-3-foot square with only two feet on the ground. This is a wonderful activity for a retreat or an extended group meeting on the topic of being friends, dealing with tough times, or leadership.

Suggested Time

15 to 20 minutes

Group Size

This strategy works with any size group, divided into small groups of up to eight people.

Special Considerations

If some of the people in your group are extremely self-conscious about their body, this exercise is likely to be uncomfortable for them. If you know this to be true of any of the young teens in your group, you might suggest that one person from each group volunteer to act as a judge and spotter for another group, to make sure that they are following the rules. This option gives the person who is extremely uncomfortable the opportunity to choose a nonthreatening role to play without calling undue attention to herself or himself.

Materials Needed

☼ 3-by-3-foot pieces of carpet or stiff paper, or a roll of masking tape

PROCEDURE

Preparation. If you are using masking tape, mark off a 3-by-3-foot square for each small group. If the groups consist of six or fewer people, reduce the size of the square to about 2½-by-2½ feet.

1. If necessary divide the participants into small groups of up to eight people. Gather each group around a 3-by-3-foot square. Explain that each group's task is to get every member in the square. Let the young people try to accomplish that goal now. They will likely all huddle into the square with little trouble. Affirm their efforts, then announce that because it was so easy for them, you are imposing a new rule: Each group can have only two feet touching the ground. That means that in a group of eight people, only two of their sixteen feet may be on the ground. The group must be able to hold that position for 10 seconds.

2. When you are certain that the young teens understand the task, tell them to begin. Emphasize that this is not a competition but a problem-solving exercise. They should not rush to be first. Instead they should look for the most creative way to solve the problem.

3. After all the groups have finished the task and are able to hold their position for 10 seconds, congratulate them for their efforts. Then lead a discussion of the following questions:

When you first heard about the new rule, what was your reaction?

How did your group come up with a solution?

What solutions did you try that did not work?

How is performing this exercise like friendship?

How is performing this exercise like being a disciple of Jesus?

4. Conclude with an affirmation of the young people's unique problem-solving skills and a prayer of thanksgiving for nimble bodies and creative minds.

ALTERNATIVE APPROACH

◎ If your group numbers around ten and you would rather not break it into smaller groups, increase the size of the square to about 4-by-4 feet and the number of feet the group can have touching the ground to three or four.

SCRIPTURAL CONNECTIONS

- ⊚ Prov. 3:21–26 (Keep forging ahead with confidence.)
- ⊚ Psalm 62 (Trust in God.)
- ⊚ 1 Cor. 12:12–31 (The body must work together.)
- ⊚ Acts 2:43–47 (Living as a Christian community)

NOTES

Use the space below to jot notes and reminders for the next time you use this strategy.

Connect the Dots

OVERVIEW

This strategy is an active variation of a mind game that has been around for a while. Young teens, however, are not likely to have seen it. It will get them thinking outside the box and trying to solve a problem together. It is a good activity for a session on leadership, making decisions, facing difficulties, or communication.

Suggested Time

15 to 20 minutes

Group Size

This strategy is designed for ten people. If your group is larger, engage the others as puzzle solvers. If your group has twenty or more people, divide the young teens into two groups and create two dot puzzles.

Materials Needed

- ☼ masking tape (optional)
- ☼ a skein of yarn or a ball of string

PROCEDURE

Preparation. You may want to use masking tape to mark nine spots on the floor, three rows of three, equally spaced so that they form a square (see the configuration of dots in step 2 below). This will save a little time at the start of the activity.

1. Recruit nine people to serve as dots. Have them sit on the floor in three rows of three, equally spaced, so that they form a square with one dot in the middle. Tell the person or people who are not dots that they are puzzle solvers. Explain their task in this way:

> Your task is to connect all nine dots using only four straight lines. The lines must be formed using only one continuous piece of yarn or string.

Do not add any other details to the instructions. Keep them basic and to the point. Ask that people who have seen this puzzle before not give away the answer. If one of the puzzle solvers says that he or she has seen this puzzle before, suggest that he or she trade places with one of the dots who has not seen the puzzle before.

2. When the puzzle solvers understand the task, let them begin. If after 10 minutes they do not look like they are close to a solution, show them the following possibilities:

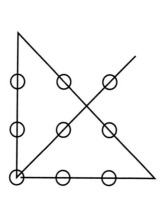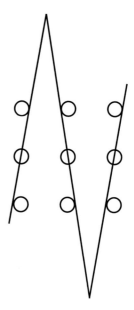

3. Lead a discussion of the following questions:

What kinds of solutions did the puzzle solvers come up with?

What did it finally take to solve this puzzle?

What surprised you about the solution?

How does this puzzle relate to problems we have to solve in everyday life?

Think of a personal, community, or world problem that could benefit from this kind of outside-the-box thinking.

In what ways was Jesus an outside-the-box thinker?

4. Close with a prayer for the guidance of the Holy Spirit so that our eyes may be opened to new ways of thinking and creative solutions.

ALTERNATIVE APPROACHES

◎ If you have fewer than ten participants, use chairs as dots and have all the teens work together to solve the problem.

◎ Select with the young people a problem that the group or class, the parish or school, or the community is dealing with. Brainstorm with them a list of solutions. Go through the ideas and identify each one as either inside the box or outside the box. Decide if any of them will get the job done and are feasible. Select one solution and work out a plan for making it a reality.

SCRIPTURAL CONNECTIONS

◎ Ps. 25:4–5 (Ask God for guidance to find the right path.)
◎ Isa. 42:16 (God leads us.)
◎ Hos. 14:9 (The wise follow the ways of the Lord.)
◎ Prov. 3:21–26 (Keep forging ahead with confidence.)
◎ 1 Cor. 12:12–31 (The body must work together.)
◎ Acts 2:43–47 (Living as a Christian community)

NOTES

Use the space below to jot notes and reminders for the next time you use this strategy.

(This strategy is adapted from *Youth Group Trust Builders,* by Denny Rydberg, pp. 28–29)

Swamp Crossing

OVERVIEW

Teams of the young people must find a way to get all their members across an alligator-infested swamp using only three pieces of cardboard as shields. This is a great problem-solving activity and can easily be incorporated into a meeting, a class, or a retreat on themes of friendship, leadership, decision making, and finding one's way through life's difficulties.

Suggested Time

About 20 minutes

Group Size

This strategy can be done with any size group, divided into small groups of five or six.

Materials Needed

- masking tape
- 8½-by-11-inch pieces of cardboard, three for each small group

PROCEDURE

Preparation. Mark off a swamp for each group by placing two strips of masking tape on the floor 10 to 12 feet apart. Put three pieces of cardboard near one end of each swamp.

1. Form small groups of five to six people each. Explain the following situation to everyone:

> Your group is on a journey. You have come to a swamp that is infested with hungry alligators that have not eaten in days, and you must find a way to get everyone in your group across. The only way to cross safely is to use the three alligator shields that are at the beginning of the swamp. You must follow certain rules:
>
>> Only one foot or other body part may be on an alligator shield at one time.
>>
>> Any body part that is not on a shield and touches the water will get consumed immediately by an alligator. You cannot use that body part for the rest of the exercise. If your entire body falls into the water, you must start over from the beginning.
>>
>> The shields may be picked up and moved to get people across, but they may not be thrown or slid across the water.

2. When you are sure that the young people understand the directions, give them a signal to start. Emphasize that this exercise is not a competition to see who finishes first. It is an exercise to see who can come up with a creative solution to the problem.

3. After the groups have completed the exercise, gather everyone and lead a discussion of the following questions:

> What solutions did people come up with?
>
> What sacrifices did people have to make to get everyone across?
>
> In real life what are the alligators that are ready to take a bite out of us as soon as we slip off the shields?
>
> Who helps us across the swamps of life?
>
> Who or what are our shields against the alligators of life?

4. Close with a prayer thanking God for the people who help us get across the swamps of life; for our faith in Jesus Christ, which helps us deal with the hurt; and for the Holy Spirit, who gives us the courage to keep on going and helps us find a way out.

ALTERNATIVE APPROACHES

- Make the task a little more complicated by giving each group a 5- to 10-pound sack of supplies to get across the swamp. The more unwieldy the sack, the better. Explain that the sack cannot come in contact with the swamp water.
- Instead of a sack of items, designate one of the lighter young teens in the group to be the supply sack. This person cannot do anything or contribute to the solution. He or she must act as an injured, unconscious person.

SCRIPTURAL CONNECTIONS

- Luke 5:17–26 (Jesus heals the paralytic.)
- Sir. 6:5–17 (The qualities of friendship)
- Col. 3:12–17 (Support and encourage one another.)
- Rom. 8:28–29 (All things work together for good.)

NOTES

Use the space below to jot notes and reminders for the next time you use this strategy.

(This strategy is adapted from *Building Community in Youth Groups,* by Denny Rydberg, pp. 48–49.)

Climbing the Walls

OVERVIEW In this strategy, the young teens work together in small groups to place a piece of tape as high on a wall as they can. Through this activity they come to know that everyone must get involved and that the person who places the tape on the wall is no more important than those who helped her or him get there.

Suggested Time

About 15 minutes

Group Size

This strategy can be done with any size group, divided into small groups of six to fifteen participants each.

Special Considerations

This activity works only in a gym or another room with a high ceiling. You will not be able to achieve the desired results in a room with a low ceiling.

Because this strategy is likely to involve people climbing on one another and reaching, be sure to have other adults around to act as spotters and to monitor the activity of each small group.

Materials Needed

- ☀ 2-inch pieces of masking tape, one for each small group

PROCEDURE

1. If you have more than fifteen people in your group, form small groups of at least six people each. You may want to use one of the grouping exercises in part A of this manual to accomplish that task.

Have each group sit together in front of the wall where the activity will take place. Explain to the young people that their task is to work with their team to place a 2-inch piece of masking tape as high on the wall as possible. They cannot use any props. They can use only the people in their group. Emphasize the need for safety and point out the people who will act as monitors and spotters. Say nothing about who from the group must be involved in achieving the goal.

Tell the teens that you will stop them in 10 minutes. If they get the tape on the wall and then think of a better way to do it, they can try again, provided they finish within the 10 minutes. Give the groups a signal to begin.

2. Stop the activity after 10 minutes. Tell the young people to stand back and decide for themselves which group's piece of tape is highest on the wall.

3. Lead a discussion of these questions:

How did your group accomplish the task? Did you engage in planning or in trial and error?

Was everyone involved in the task? If so, how was each individual involved? If not, why not?

Who was the most important person in achieving the goal?

What did you learn about being a team during this exercise?

How was this exercise like the situation in our parish or school?

How was performing this exercise like being a Christian?

4. Close the exercise by emphasizing the importance of everyone contributing what they can to the work of a community, whether it be a family, a class, a parish, or the whole church. Point out that no one person on a team was more important than any other in accomplishing the task, including the spotter, who played an important role.

End with a prayer that we all keep reaching for our goals and that we have the strength of character to help other people reach theirs. Pray, too, that we all work together to make the Reign of God real here and now.

SCRIPTURAL CONNECTIONS

- ◎ 2 Tim. 1:6–10 (God gave us a spirit of power, not of cowardice.)
- ◎ Phil. 4:8–9 (The virtues of living life in Christ)
- ◎ Phil. 3:13–16 (Press on toward the goal.)

NOTES

Use the space below to jot notes and reminders for the next time you use this strategy.

(This strategy is adapted from *Building Community in Youth Groups,* by Denny Rydberg, pp. 36–37.)

Five More Team Builders

OVERVIEW The activities listed in this section encompass many different ideas, but can be grouped into five categories: playing, cooking, planning, serving, and praying. Millions of words have been written in youth ministry manuals in the last twenty-five years summarizing thousands of ideas in each of those categories. See the bibliography in the introduction of this book for helpful resources to consult for more ideas.

Suggested Time

The time required for each of these activities varies. A simple relay could be over in 5 minutes. A cookie-baking session could last an afternoon.

Group Size

The strategies summarized in this section will work with any size group.

SUGGESTED STRATEGIES

On Your Mark: Playing

Games are a wonderful way to teach young teens about working together, about being a team, about strengths and weaknesses, about functioning under pressure, about success and failure, about being church, and about life in general. Relays are always good because they are quick, active, and involve everyone. Everyone shares in the victory or the defeat. Simulations are helpful for building teams because they involve working together on a problem and coming up with a solution together; they are also an easy way to find out individuals' strengths and weaknesses. Board games or box games are another way of building community among groups of young teens. Particularly helpful are games that pit team against team. Young teens can have hours of fun with games that challenge them as individuals and as a team, and come away feeling closer to one another.

Someone's in the Kitchen: Cooking

Young teens enjoy food. And almost as much as they enjoy eating food, they enjoy making food. Being allowed to cook is still a new thing to most of them, and they are happy to contribute what they can to cooking projects. Whether it's soup for a parish Lenten supper, pancakes for a parish breakfast, cookies for a local women's shelter, pizza from scratch for a lock-in, or a 20-foot ice cream sundae, they work well together in a supervised environment and take great pride in their accomplishments. Be sure to have enough adult helpers to answer questions and monitor the activity.

What Should We Do? Planning

Young teens can be highly creative if given the chance. Their imaginations are still vivid, and generally have not been squelched by more formal types of learning. Many young teens still have the types of imagination that adults work hard to recapture. Put them together to plan a prayer service, and they may surprise you with their depth and sincerity. They can excel at skits and role-plays, and they can touch even the hardest heart in their modern interpretations of Gospel stories. Set them on an information trail and challenge them to present it to the group creatively, and they are likely to come up with information that is hard to forget. Working together on such projects can bring a group of young teens close and build a sense of unity and an appreciation of one another's giftedness.

Can I Help You? Serving

Young teens need to be needed. They have a tremendous capacity for caring, an eye for injustice, and a mind and body capable of doing more than they are often given credit for. Perhaps the surest way to form a sense of team among young adolescents is to set them in the direction of helping someone else. It is also the surest way to build their sense of self-esteem, their idea of what being church is all about, and their commitment to discipleship. After all, when they serve others, they are doing exactly what Jesus asks them to do.

Whether your young teens are helping out on Sunday mornings in the parish nursery, stringing Christmas lights on a community landmark, raising funds and collecting children's books for the local homeless shelter, cleaning up local hiking trails, trick-or-treating for the hungry, or participating in any number of other service projects, the benefits are numerous and widespread.

Dear God: Praying

Despite what many adults think about them, young teens like to pray. They may not always show it, but they are deeply spiritual people—in their own way. They like prayer times when they are invited to journey in their imagination to a place where they are alone with God. They like prayer times when they are invited—but not forced—to share what is in their heart with others. They like prayer times that are rich in symbolism and ritual, particularly those that are created especially for them and those that they help create. They enjoy stories that lead to prayer, music that leads to prayer, and silence that leads to prayer. They enjoy telling one another stories, singing music together, and being with one another in silence. All those things bring a group of young teens closer together, in the knowledge that they come together as gifts to the world and to one another from a loving Creator.

NOTES

Use the space below to jot notes and reminders for the next time you use these strategies.

Part E
Affirming One Another

Affirming someone is a difficult skill to learn, no matter how old a person is. The affirmation must be sincere and specific so that the person being affirmed knows exactly what is special about her or him. Young teens need to learn this valuable skill. They also need to be on the receiving end of such affirmation, from their peers and from adults, because even the most self-assured young adolescent has self-doubt much of the time.

The strategies in part E help facilitate the process of affirming young teens and helping them affirm one another. Affirmation is one of the most important elements in building a sense of community—letting people know that they belong, that their gifts are appreciated, and that they are lovable and loved.

Bag of Goodies

OVERVIEW The young people give candy to one another, offering with each piece an analogy between the candy and the gifts of the recipient.

Suggested Time

About 10 minutes, depending on the size of the group

Group Size

This strategy is intended for a group of about twenty participants. If your group is larger than that, divide the young teens into smaller groups.

Materials Needed

- ☼ a bag
- ☼ a wide assortment of wrapped candy, at least one piece for each person

PROCEDURE

Gather the young teens in a circle. Pass a bag of wrapped candy around the group, and tell the participants to take one candy from the bag and hold on to it. When everyone has a candy, invite them one at a time to give their candy away to someone in the circle. As they do so, they are to tell the person why he or she reminds them of the candy, by completing the following statement:

_____ [Name of person], you are like _____ [name of candy] because _____ [reason].

Emphasize that all the statements need to be positive. You may need to give some examples such as the following ones:

Charlie, you are like this pack of Smarties because you came up with a brilliant idea for that puzzle we had to solve.

Jasmine, you are like this piece of bubble gum because you really stuck to the task until we found a solution.

Garrett, you are like this Tootsie Roll Pop because you're full of surprises.

If a person receives more than one piece of candy, he or she must give it to someone else, along with an affirmation—until everyone in the room has a piece of candy and an affirmation to go with it.

ALTERNATIVE APPROACH

◎ Instead of letting each person draw one candy from a bag, give each person a sandwich bag with five or six candies in it. Tell everyone that they must walk around the room and give away all their candies, using the same formula outlined above. They can receive candy from others, but they must give away anything over eight pieces.

NOTES

Use the space below to jot notes and reminders for the next time you use this strategy.

(This strategy is adapted from *No-Miss Lessons for Preteen Kids*, by the editors of Group Publishing, p. 33.)

Balloon Affirmations

OVERVIEW In this strategy the young people use balloons as the vehicle for their affirmations of one another.

Suggested Time

About 10 minutes, depending on the size of the group

Group Size

This strategy works with any size group.

Materials Needed

- ☼ small pieces of paper, about 3-by-3 inches, one for each person
- ☼ pens or pencils
- ☼ a bag or a basket
- ☼ balloons, one for each person and a few extras
- ☼ a tape or CD player, and an appropriate recording (optional)
- ☼ a few straight pins

PROCEDURE

1. Give everyone a piece of paper, and a pen or a pencil. Tell them to write their name on one side of the paper and fold it up. Collect the papers in a bag or a basket.

2. Tell the participants that as you pass the bag or the basket around the group, each person should take out one piece of paper and read it but not let anyone know whose name he or she picked. As the names are being picked, also give each person a balloon.

3. Direct the young teens to think about the person whose name they chose and to write one positive thing about that person on the back of the paper. If possible they should be specific in what they are praising the person for. However, if they do not know the person well, it is fine simply to say something like, "You're fun to be around."

When they finish writing the compliment, they should roll the paper into a thin cylinder, insert it into the balloon, blow the balloon up, and tie it off.

4. When everyone has tied their balloons, tell them to stand up and toss the balloons in the air. The goal is to keep all the balloons in the air. During this time you may want to play an appropriate upbeat song about friendship or being there for one another.

5. After a few minutes, announce that everyone should take one balloon and sit in a circle. They do not need to find their original balloon. Tell them to pop their balloon and take out the paper. Make a few straight pins available to help with this task.

When everyone has a paper from a balloon, invite the young teens to read the name on the paper and the affirmation that someone in the group wrote about that person. Someone may have deliberately written something negative—knowing that the source of the comment is likely to remain anonymous—so caution the group members not to read such comments aloud. If something negative does get said about someone, try to counter the effect of the statement by asking others in the group to offer positive comments about that person.

6. Thank the young people for their cooperation, and challenge them to keep one another from hitting the ground by treating each person they meet with respect and appreciation.

ALTERNATIVE APPROACH

◉ If you have a small group, you may want to give each person two sheets of paper and two balloons, to make the balloon-batting part of the strategy more challenging and offer double the number of affirmations.

NOTES

Use the space below to jot notes and reminders for the next time you use this strategy.

(This strategy is adapted from *Youth Group Trust Builders,* by Denny Rydberg, pp. 85–86.)

First Corinthians Affirmations

This strategy is based on 1 Cor. 12:12–27 (The body is one and has many members). The teens affirm one another by giving awards based on how each person acts as a part of the Body of Christ.

Suggested Time

About 20 minutes, depending on the size of the group

Group Size

This strategy works well with groups of up to twenty-five people.

Materials Needed

- a Bible
- newsprint and markers

PROCEDURE

1. Ask for a volunteer to read 1 Cor. 12:12–27. Discuss the meaning of the passage with the participants, focusing on the likening of the human body to the Body of Christ and the important role that every part plays in it.

2. List on newsprint several parts of the body: eye, ear, mouth, head, foot, hand, heart, brain, and so forth. Ask the young people to name the functions of those parts of the body. In other words, how do the specific parts of the body contribute to the smooth functioning of the body as a whole? Write their ideas next to the part of the body.

3. One by one, ask the participants to sit in the middle or in front of the group. Invite everyone else to assign a part of the body to this person and give a reason for doing so. For example, they might say something like, "Marty, you are like an ear because you listen to people" or "Olivia, you are like a hand because you are always helping others."

4. Close by thanking the young people for their cooperation and reminding them of their importance to your group and to the Body of Christ.

ALTERNATIVE APPROACHES

- Recruit a group of young teens to act out the passage from Corinthians. You would probably need to ask them several days before your meeting and work with them to prepare a skit.
- If you think that your group will be reluctant to share affirmations aloud, consider having only the adults do affirmations. Allow the young teens to add their ideas if they wish to.
- If you have a small group or lots of time, try this variation: Instead of having the young people offer verbal affirmations, give everyone a sheet of self-stick mailing labels with the participants' names already printed on them. Each person should write a part of the body on each label and a word or two about why he or she associated that person with that part of the body. Post a sheet of construction paper for each person on the wall, labeling it with that person's name. Have the young teens affix their labels to the appropriate sheets. When everyone has completed the task, give the young teens time to read their own sheet. Afterward, let them take it home.

NOTES

Use the space below to jot notes and reminders for the next time you use this strategy.

I Give You This Gift

In this strategy the young people give their peers imaginary gifts, based on what they know about one another. This affirmation is likely to work best with teens at the upper end of middle school or those who know one another fairly well and are comfortable with one another. It makes an ideal end-of-the-year activity or retreat activity.

Suggested Time

Anywhere from 10 to 60 minutes, depending on how elaborate the young people get

Group Size

This strategy works with any size group.

Materials Needed

- ☼ paper lunch bags, one for each person
- ☼ markers
- ☼ masking tape
- ☼ blank paper in a variety of colors and sizes
- ☼ pens or pencils
- ☼ a tape or CD player, and a recording of reflective music (optional)

PROCEDURE

1. Hand out paper lunch bags and markers and direct everyone to write their name on the front of a bag and tape it to a wall.

2. Make a wide variety of papers, and pens or pencils available to the young people. Tell them that they are to give each person in the group an imaginary gift. It should not be an actual gift, but a note describing something they wish they could give that person, based on what they know about him or her. For example, they might say, "Julia, because I know you want to see different places in the world, I give you a gift of unlimited airline travel" or "Steve, I know you are a talented artist. I give you the gift of all the art supplies you need for a lifetime, and people who appreciate what you do" or "Mike, if I could, I would give you a special mirror so that you can see yourself as others do."

If your group is small, let everyone give a gift to everyone else. If your group is large and has been working in smaller teams, let the participants give a gift to everyone else on their team. If your group is large and has not been working in small groups, put everyone's name on a separate slip of paper, put the slips in a bag, and let each person draw out a name to determine whom they should give a gift to.

Request that they work quietly and prayerfully, thinking about the gift that would be most appropriate for each person. You may want to play a recording of reflective music while they are doing this.

3. When they finish their notes, they should put them in the recipient's bag on the wall. Give the young people a chance to read the notes they receive and let them take the notes home at the end of the session.

ALTERNATIVE APPROACHES

◎ If you have an extended amount of time, make a variety of craft supplies available and encourage the young people to decorate their bag.

◎ If you are doing this exercise as part of a retreat or an extended session, direct the young people to create personal collages on the bags, thus combining a get-to-know-you activity with an affirmation activity.

◎ To save time you may want to make out gift certificates that the young people can just fill in. They should say something like, "_____ [Name of person], if I could, I would give you the gift of _____ [type of gift] because _____ [reason]."

NOTES

Use the space below to jot notes and reminders for the next time you use this strategy.

Compliment Contest

OVERVIEW

This strategy starts by establishing a put-down–free zone, gives the young teens some tools to build up one another, and challenges them to say as many complimentary things to one another as they can. It is especially effective as an opening activity for an extended meeting or event.

Suggested Time

About 10 minutes

Group Size

This strategy works with any size group, divided into small groups of six to eight people.

Materials Needed

- ☼ one sheet of poster board in a bold or neon color
- ☼ markers
- ☼ masking tape
- ☼ newsprint, one sheet for each small group
- ☼ small prizes (optional)

PROCEDURE

Preparation. On poster board make a large sign that says, "Put-down–free zone," and post it in a place where it will be visible. The bolder and brighter the sign, the better.

1. When the young people gather, call their attention to the sign that says, "Put-down–free zone." Announce that you want them not only to refrain from putting people down but also to concentrate on actively building up people.

2. Form small groups of six to eight people. Give each group a sheet of newsprint and a variety of markers. Challenge the groups to list as many ways to build up people as they can think of in 3 minutes. You may want to give examples such as the following:

That was a great idea!

I couldn't have done it without you.

You've got a wonderful way of making people feel comfortable.

Give them a signal to begin.

3. After 3 minutes call time. Invite the groups to post their newsprint in the front of the room. Read the lists of ways to build up people. Encourage the young teens to use those and other ideas frequently throughout the meeting or event. Caution them to take the challenge seriously and to give sincere compliments to one another.

You may want to provide small prizes at the end of the session or event, to those who have been the most complimentary throughout.

ALTERNATIVE APPROACH

◎ Appoint a few people to be "compliment police" and explain to them that their job is to catch someone saying something nice to someone else. Suggest that they keep a list of who said what and report at the end of the meeting or event. With this option the compliment givers end up getting complimented.

NOTES

Use the space below to jot notes and reminders for the next time you use this strategy.

(This strategy is adapted from *Growing Close,* edited by Stephen Parolini, p. 23.)

You're Respect-a-Ball!

The young people toss around a beach ball while telling one another why they are worthy and deserving of respect and kindness. This activity is a good way to help young teens understand the concept of respect and how respect differs from compliments.

Suggested Time

10 minutes

Group Size

This activity works best with a group of up to fifteen people. If your group is larger than that, use more than one beach ball and recruit adults to help monitor the activity.

Special Considerations

Very young adolescents may be reluctant to elaborate on a concept as nebulous as respect. If you have many participants who are age ten, eleven, or twelve, you may want to use the alternative approach offered near the end of this strategy.

Materials Needed

- ☼ beach balls, preferably without any printing or pictures on them, one for every fifteen people
- ☼ permanent markers, one for every fifteen people

PROCEDURE

1. Ask the young people what the word *respect* means. Chances are they will know the basic meaning of the word. Elicit from them how respecting someone differs from giving them a compliment. Be sure to draw out these ideas: We *compliment* someone because of what they have done or accomplished. We *respect* everyone because of who they are as human beings. All human beings have the right to be respected.

2. Put in the middle of the group one beach ball for every fifteen participants. Invite the young teens to offer several reasons that we respect people. As they offer their reasons, have the young people write them on the beach ball using a permanent marker. Be sure that in the end, the following reasons are represented in some form:
◎ God created everyone.
◎ We are made in the image and likeness of God.
◎ All human beings are entitled to basic dignity and respect.
◎ Respect is the foundation of all human relationships.
◎ Human beings naturally strive for goodness. In those efforts they must be respected and supported.

3. Toss a beach ball to someone, and as you do tell that person why you respect her or him. For example, you might say, "I respect you because I know you care about others" or "I respect you because I see you doing God's work." Invite the young teens to do the same for one another. Make sure everyone gets a ball at some point.

4. Close with a challenge to respect all people at all times—whether or not we like a particular person. Respecting has nothing to do with liking. We owe people respect no matter who they are in our eyes. What counts is who they are in God's eyes.

ALTERNATIVE APPROACH

◎ If you have many people under age thirteen in your group, consider omitting personal expressions of respect in step 3. Instead, suggest that the young people read from the ball a reason to respect others and then toss the ball to someone who has not yet had it, continuing until all the reasons have been read.

NOTES

Use the space below to jot notes and reminders for the next time you use this strategy.

Spin the Compliment

OVERVIEW

This strategy is like the popular party game spin the bottle, with a new twist. The young teens take turns spinning a bottle and giving an affirmation to the person the bottle points at when it comes to rest.

Suggested Time

About 10 minutes

Group Size

This exercise works well with up to fifteen people. If your group is larger than that, you may want to divide the participants into smaller groups and provide a separate bottle for each group.

Materials Needed

☼ an empty plastic or glass soda bottle

PROCEDURE

Gather the young people in a circle and put the empty bottle on its side in the middle of the circle. Tell the young teens that they are going to take turns spinning the bottle in the middle of the circle. The person who spins the bottle must give a compliment or say a few words of affirmation or encouragement to the person the bottle is pointing to when it stops. Assure them that they do not need to speak for a long time; a simple phrase or one sentence will suffice.

Begin the process yourself to set the tone. After you are finished, the person who just received the affirmation spins the bottle and offers a few words to the person it points to, and so forth. If the bottle points to someone who has already had a turn, have the spinner spin again. Follow this pattern until everyone has given and received affirmation.

ALTERNATIVE APPROACH

◎ Invite other people to offer affirmation and encouragement to the recipient after the spinner has had her or his chance to do so.

NOTES

Use the space below to jot notes and reminders for the next time you use this strategy.

(This strategy is adapted from *More Attention Grabbers for Fourth–Sixth Graders,* by David Lynn, p. 71.)

Acrostic Affirmations

The young people receive written affirmations from others in the form of an acrostic that uses the letters of their name. This is a good affirmation activity for young teens who might be reluctant to affirm others verbally.

Suggested Time

5 to 15 minutes, depending on the size of the group

Group Size

This strategy works best with up to twenty people. If your group is larger than that, you may want to divide the participants into smaller groups.

Materials Needed

- lined notebook paper, one piece for each person
- pens or pencils

PROCEDURE

1. Invite everyone to be seated in a circle and give them each a sheet of notebook paper, and a pen or a pencil. Tell them to write their first name down the left side of the paper, one letter on every other line. Suggest that people with short first names may want to use their first and last names. For example, a girl with the name Elizabeth would only use her first name. But a boy named Jay Kloc might use his first and last names. The idea is to maximize the affirmation potential of each person's name.

2. When everyone has written their name on their paper, direct them to pass it one person to the left. The recipient of the paper must write an affirmation or a positive characteristic about the person whose name is on the paper, and it must begin with a letter of the person's name and be written on the same line as that letter. Tell the young people to continue passing the papers to the left and writing on each one that comes to them until they receive their own. Suggest that if someone receives a paper on which all the letters of a person's name have been used, they may reuse one of the letters by adding a word or phrase behind what is already written there. A completed paper might look like this:

Bright ideas
Really good listener
I like to be around him
Always helpful
Not afraid to speak up

Give the young people a chance to read their papers. Thank them for their honest support of one another.

ALTERNATIVE APPROACH

◎ If you are doing this as part of a retreat or an extended session, try this option: Instead of doing this activity all at once in a circle, have the young people post their name sheet on a wall. Encourage others to go to the wall periodically throughout the retreat or session and write an affirmation of someone. Monitor the results to make sure that everyone's paper is getting attention.

NOTES

Use the space below to jot notes and reminders for the next time you use this strategy.

(This strategy is adapted from *More Attention Grabbers for Fourth–Sixth Graders,* by David Lynn, p. 69.)

A Pat on the Back

OVERVIEW

The young people write affirmations and words of encouragement on papers that are pinned to people's backs. This is a good exercise for young teens who may by shy about saying things to people face-to-face.

Suggested Time

5 to 10 minutes, depending on the size of the group

Group Size

This strategy works with any size group.

Materials Needed

- ☼ 8½-by-11-inch paper, one piece for each person
- ☼ pens or pencils
- ☼ straight pins, one for each person

PROCEDURE

1. Gather the young people in a circle. Distribute to everyone a sheet of paper and a pencil or a pen and tell them to write their name on the top of the paper.

2. Give each person a straight pin. Tell everyone to turn to the person on their right and pin their neighbor's name sheet onto his or her back, between the shoulder blades. Caution them to be careful with the pin and to fasten it securely so that it does not move and prick the person.

3. Announce that everyone is to mingle and write positive comments about people on their sheet. If they have been working in small groups, encourage them to write something for every person in their small group. Monitor the results to make sure that everyone's paper is getting attention.

4. After the allotted time, ask the young people to unpin the sheets from one another's clothing and give them to their owner. Allow the young teens a few minutes to read the things people wrote about them.

ALTERNATIVE APPROACH

◎ This activity can be done in a more structured fashion that still ensures a degree of anonymity. Gather the young teens in a circle. Have each person write her or his name across the top of a sheet of paper. Pass the papers to the right. The person who now holds the paper writes a positive comment at the bottom of the paper, folds it upward, and passes it to the next person, who writes a comment on the bottom, folds it upward, and passes it along. This process continues until each person's paper is full of affirming comments.

NOTES

Use the space below to jot notes and reminders for the next time you use this strategy.

Alphabetical Affirmations

The young people and the adults create for each person in the group a poster filled with affirming characteristics that correspond to each letter of the alphabet. It makes a wonderfully affirming poster to take home at the end of a course or semester. This is a good strategy to use over an extended period of time if you have a wall that you can leave covered with posters.

Suggested Time

This strategy is best done over several weeks.

Group Size

This strategy works with any size group.

Materials Needed

- ☼ sheets of poster board, one for each person
- ☼ a variety of markers
- ☼ old magazines and catalogs, scissors, glue sticks, and other craft supplies (optional)
- ☼ masking tape or poster tape

PROCEDURE

1. Give each person a sheet of poster board and provide a variety of markers. Tell everyone to write their name in bold letters at the top of their poster board. Encourage them to be as creative as possible. You may want to make available magazines and other craft supplies. After they write their name, tell them to write the letters of the alphabet down the left side of the poster. They should make the letters big enough so that the alphabet covers the entire left side.

After everyone finishes their work, use masking tape or poster tape to secure each poster to the wall at a level that is within easy reach for all the participants.

2. Announce that the posters will remain on the wall for a certain amount of time. Explain to the young people that for each person in the group, they are to think of positive things to say that each correspond to a letter of the alphabet. Then they should add each word or phrase to that person's poster beside the corresponding letter. They should write something on every person's poster before it is time to take the posters down. Encourage them to fill in blank spots on a person's poster before doubling up on any letters that are already used. Monitor the results to make sure that everyone's paper is getting attention.

Encourage the adults involved with the group, yourself included, to add their comments to the posters as well.

3. At the end of the allotted time, give the young people their poster to take home. Encourage them to put the poster up in their room to remind them that they are good people.

ALTERNATIVE APPROACH

◎ Plan a prayer service for the meeting or class that marks the end of the affirmation period. During that service present the posters to the young people. As part of the presentation, have everyone in the group enthusiastically read aloud each person's poster together, from *A* to *Z*, while that person holds it. For the participants the effect of an entire group of peers shouting nice things about them will likely remain a fond memory for a long while. If the group is large, spread the reading out over several days.

NOTES

Use the space below to jot notes and reminders for the next time you use this strategy.

(This strategy is adapted from *101 Affirmations for Teenagers,* compiled by the editors of Group Publishing, p. 13.)

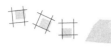

Appendix 1

Connections to the Discovering Program by HELP Strategy

Most of the strategies in this book have broad application to any course in the Discovering Program or any other religious education program. However, the strategies in part D, "Building Teams," are longer, are more developed, and in many cases have a more specific tie-in to a particular catechetical theme. Because of that the connections listed below apply only to part D of this book.

"Blind Lineup"

This strategy complements the following Discovering courses:
◎ *Becoming Friends*
◎ *Dealing with Tough Times*
◎ *Exploring the Bible*
◎ *Exploring the Story of Israel*
◎ *Learning to Communicate*
◎ *Making Decisions*
◎ *Seeking Justice*
◎ *Understanding Myself*

"Human Sculptures"

This strategy complements the following Discovering courses:
- *Becoming Friends*
- *Being Catholic*
- *Dealing with Tough Times*
- *Gathering to Celebrate*
- *Learning to Communicate*
- *Understanding Myself*

"Over the Wall"

This strategy complements the following Discovering courses:
- *Becoming Friends*
- *Being Catholic*
- *Dealing with Tough Times*
- *Learning to Communicate*
- *Making Decisions*
- *Understanding Myself*

"Spaghetti Towers"

This strategy complements the following courses in the Discovering Program:
- *Being Catholic*
- *Gathering to Celebrate*
- *Learning to Communicate*
- *Making Decisions*
- *Seeking Justice*
- *Understanding Myself*

"Jesus Jingles"

This strategy complements the following courses in the Discovering Program:
- *Being Catholic*
- *Celebrating the Eucharist*
- *Exploring the Bible*
- *Gathering to Celebrate*
- *Meeting Jesus*
- *Praying*

"Yert Circle"

This strategy complements the following courses in the Discovering Program:
- *Becoming Friends*
- *Being Catholic*
- *Dealing with Tough Times*
- *Gathering to Celebrate*
- *Seeking Justice*
- *Understanding Myself*

"Group Juggling"

This strategy complements the following courses in the Discovering Program:
- *Becoming Friends*
- *Being Catholic*
- *Dealing with Tough Times*
- *Growing Up Sexually*
- *Learning to Communicate*

"Look Very Closely"

This strategy complements the following courses in the Discovering Program:
- *Becoming Friends*
- *Exploring the Bible*
- *Learning to Communicate*
- *Making Decisions*
- *Praying*

"Stand in the Square"

This strategy complements the following courses in the Discovering Program:
- *Becoming Friends*
- *Being Catholic*
- *Dealing with Tough Times*
- *Growing Up Sexually*
- *Learning to Communicate*
- *Making Decisions*
- *Meeting Jesus*
- *Understanding Myself*

"Connect the Dots"

This strategy complements the following Discovering courses:

- ◎ *Dealing with Tough Times*
- ◎ *Learning to Communicate*
- ◎ *Making Decisions*
- ◎ *Seeking Justice*

"Swamp Crossing"

This strategy complements the following courses in the Discovering Program:

- ◎ *Becoming Friends*
- ◎ *Being Catholic*
- ◎ *Dealing with Tough Times*
- ◎ *Learning to Communicate*
- ◎ *Making Decisions*
- ◎ *Meeting Jesus*
- ◎ *Seeking Justice*

"Climbing the Walls"

This strategy complements the following Discovering courses:

- ◎ *Becoming Friends*
- ◎ *Being Catholic*
- ◎ *Celebrating the Eucharist*
- ◎ *Dealing with Tough Times*
- ◎ *Gathering to Celebrate*
- ◎ *Making Decisions*
- ◎ *Seeking Justice*

Appendix 2

Connections to the Discovering Program by Discovering Course

Most of the strategies in this book have broad application to any course in the Discovering Program or any other religious education program. However, the strategies in part D, "Building Teams," are longer, are more developed, and in many cases have a more specific tie-in to a particular catechetical theme. Because of that the connections listed below apply only to part D of this book.

Becoming Friends

These HELP strategies complement this course as they are presented:
◎ "Blind Lineup"
◎ "Human Sculptures"
◎ "Over the Wall"
◎ "Yert Circle"
◎ "Group Juggling"
◎ "Look Very Closely"
◎ "Stand in the Square"
◎ "Swamp Crossing"
◎ "Climbing the Walls"

Being Catholic

These HELP strategies complement this course as they are presented:
- "Human Sculptures"
- "Over the Wall"
- "Spaghetti Towers"
- "Jesus Jingles"
- "Yert Circle"
- "Group Juggling"
- "Stand in the Square"
- "Swamp Crossing"
- "Climbing the Walls"

Celebrating the Eucharist

These HELP strategies complement this course as they are presented:
- "Jesus Jingles"
- "Climbing the Walls"

Dealing with Tough Times

These HELP strategies complement this course as they are presented:
- "Blind Lineup"
- "Human Sculptures"
- "Over the Wall"
- "Yert Circle"
- "Group Juggling"
- "Stand in the Square"
- "Connect the Dots"
- "Swamp Crossing"
- "Climbing the Walls"

Exploring the Bible

These HELP strategies complement this course as they are presented:
- "Blind Lineup"
- "Jesus Jingles"
- "Look Very Closely"

Exploring the Story of Israel

This HELP strategy complements this course as it is presented:
- "Blind Lineup"

Gathering to Celebrate

These HELP strategies complement this course as they are presented:
- "Human Sculptures"
- "Spaghetti Towers"
- "Jesus Jingles"
- "Yert Circle"
- "Climbing the Walls"

Growing Up Sexually

These HELP strategies complement this course as they are presented:
- "Group Juggling"
- "Stand in the Square"

Learning to Communicate

These HELP strategies complement this course as they are presented:
- "Human Sculptures"
- "Over the Wall"
- "Spaghetti Towers"
- "Group Juggling"
- "Look Very Closely"
- "Stand in the Square"
- "Connect the Dots"
- "Swamp Crossing"

Making Decisions

These HELP strategies complement this course as they are presented:
- "Blind Lineup"
- "Over the Wall"
- "Spaghetti Towers"
- "Look Very Closely"
- "Stand in the Square"
- "Connect the Dots"
- "Swamp Crossing"
- "Climbing the Walls"

Meeting Jesus

These HELP strategies complement this course as they are presented:
- ◎ "Jesus Jingles"
- ◎ "Stand in the Square"
- ◎ "Swamp Crossing"

Praying

These HELP strategies complement this course as they are presented:
- ◎ "Jesus Jingles"
- ◎ "Look Very Closely"

Seeking Justice

These HELP strategies complement this course as they are presented:
- ◎ "Blind Lineup"
- ◎ "Spaghetti Towers"
- ◎ "Yert Circle"
- ◎ "Connect the Dots"
- ◎ "Swamp Crossing"
- ◎ "Climbing the Walls"

Understanding Myself

These HELP strategies complement this course as they are presented:
- ◎ "Human Sculptures"
- ◎ "Over the Wall"
- ◎ "Spaghetti Towers"
- ◎ "Yert Circle"
- ◎ "Stand in the Square"

Acknowledgments (continued)

The scriptural quotation marked NAB is from the New American Bible with revised Psalms and revised New Testament. Copyright © 1991, 1986, and 1970 by the Confraternity of Christian Doctrine, 3211 Fourth Street NE, Washington, DC 20017. All rights reserved.

All other scriptural quotations contained herein are from the New Revised Standard Version of the Bible. Copyright © 1989 by the Division of Christian Education of the National Council of the Churches of Christ in the United States of America. All rights reserved.

The strategies "It's a Match" and "Comic Strip Capers" in part A and "Spin the Compliment" and "Acrostic Affirmations" in part E are adapted from More Attention Grabbers for Fourth–Sixth Graders, by David Lynn (El Cajon, CA: Youth Specialties, 1991), pages 21, 25–26, 71, and 69, respectively. Copyright © 1991 by Youth Specialties.

The strategies "It's in the Cards" and "Phrase Match" in part A are adapted from Attention Grabbers for Fourth–Sixth Graders, by David Lynn (El Cajon, CA: Youth Specialties, 1990), pages 26–27 and 23–24. Copyright © 1990 by Youth Specialties.

The English proverb and the quotation by Ralph Waldo Emerson on page 31 are from Bartlett's Familiar Quotations, 14th edition, by John Bartlett (Boston: Little, Brown and Company, 1968). Copyright © 1937 by Little, Brown and Company.

The strategy "Fifty Ways to Choose a Leader" in part A is adapted from Ideas, number 40, edited by Wayne Rice and Paul Thigpen (El Cajon, CA: Youth Specialties, 1986), page 34. Copyright © 1986 by Youth Specialties.

The strategy "On a Typical Day" in part B is adapted from Mix It Up! Creative Crowdbreakers for Youth Groups, by Les Christie et al. (Elgin, IL: David C. Cook Publishing Co., 1993), page 19. Copyright © 1993 by David C. Cook Publishing.

The strategies "Junk Mixer" and "Expectations Autographs" in part B are adapted from First Impressions: Unforgettable Openings for Youth Meetings, compiled by Pamela J. Shoup (Loveland, CO: Group Publishing, 1998), page 72 and pages 66–67 and 68. Copyright © 1998 by Group Publishing.

The activity "Name-Tag Autographs" in part B is adapted from Creative Crowd-Breakers, Mixers, and Games, compiled by Wayne Rice and Mike Yaconelli (Winona, MN: Saint Mary's Press, 1991), page 30. Copyright © 1991 by Saint Mary's Press. All rights reserved.

The strategies "Crazy Crossing" in part B, "Shed a Little Light" in part C, and "Compliment Contest" in part E are adapted from Growing Close: Activities for Building Friendships and Unity in Youth Groups, edited by Stephen Parolini (Loveland, CO: Group Publishing, 1996), pages 24, 53–54, and 23, respectively. Copyright © 1996 by Group Publishing.

Diocesan Resource Center

1551 Tenth Avenue E

Seattle, WA 98102-0126